IF GOD BE FOR US

IF GOD BE FOR US

A Collection of Sermons

C. E. B. Cranfield

Emeritus Professor of Theology
University of Durham

T. & T. Clark Ltd.,
59 George Street, Edinburgh

Copyright © T. & T. Clark Ltd., 1985

Typeset by C. R. Barber & Partners (Highlands) Ltd.,
Fort William, Scotland,
printed and bound by Page Bros (Norwich) Ltd., England,

for
T. & T. CLARK LTD
EDINBURGH

First Printed 1985

British Library Cataloguing in Publication Data

Cranfield, C.E.B.
    If God be for us: a collection of sermons.
    1. United Reformed Church—Sermons
    I. Title
    252'.05232   BX9890.U256

    ISBN 0-567-29126-X

To

RUTH

CONTENTS

PART I
A RANSOM FOR MANY

PART II
THE GOOD SAMARITAN AND OTHER SERMONS

ACKNOWLEDGEMENTS

Part I was issued in 1963 as a 'Lent book' within the then Presbyterian Church of England and Congregational Union of England and Wales. It is republished in the hope that it may thus be able to say to a wider public things which are quite as relevant now as they were then. Grateful acknowledgement is due to the United Reformed Church for permission to do this. Acknowledgement is again due to the editors and publishers of the *Scottish Journal of Theology* for permission to make use in I.6 of some material which had already appeared in their journal, and to the Oxford University Press, the Methodist Conference Office, and the S.C.M. Press, for permission to include material from *The Church Hymnary* (2nd edition), *The Methodist Hymn-Book* (1933), and F. L. Battles' translation of Calvin's *Institutes*, respectively. Two collects from *The Book of Common Prayer*, which is Crown copyright, were reprinted by permission.

In connexion with Part II, grateful acknowledgement is made to the Rev. John Stacey and the Epworth Press for permission to include sermons 1, 2 and 3, which appeared in *The Service of God* (1965), and to the Rev. Dr. R. J. W. Bevan and Messrs. A. R. Mowbray and Co., Ltd. for allowing the reprinting of sermon 4 from R. J. W. Bevan (ed.), *The Christian Way Explained* (1964). Sermon 1 was originally published· in *Theology Today* 11 (1954), pp. 368–372; 5 in *Interpretation* 19 (1965), pp. 163–167; 6 in *Communio Viatorum* 12 (1969), pp. 191–195; and 7 in *Kingsmen* No. 35 (1981), pp. 25–29. To the editors and publishers of these periodicals grateful thanks are expressed.

In biblical quotations the Revised Version (to which the American Standard Version corresponds) has been preferred for the sake of its closeness to the original. Its use of italics for words without equivalent in the original, added in order to complete the sense, has been reproduced in the texts preceding the sermons; but in the quotations within the sermons it has been ignored in order to avoid possible confusion with the use of italics for other purposes.

PART I

A Ransom for Many

1

A RANSOM FOR MANY

And Jesus called them to him, and saith unto them,
Ye know that they which are accounted to rule over
the Gentiles lord it over them; and their great ones
exercise authority over them. But it is not so among
you: but whosoever would become great among
you, shall be your minister: and whosoever would be
first among you, shall be servant of all. For verily the
Son of man came not to be ministered unto, but to
minister, and to give his life a ransom for many.

(Mark 10.42–45.)

James and John, the sons of Zebedee, had approached
Jesus with a request. They wanted Him to promise them
that, when He should come into His royal glory, they
should have the chief places of honour beside Him, the
one on His right hand and the other on His left. It is
scarcely surprising that the other disciples, when they
heard about this, were indignant with James and John.

So Jesus called His disciples to Him, and said to them:
'Ye know that they which are accounted to rule over the
Gentiles lord it over them; and their great ones exercise
authority over them.' The two Greek verbs represented by
'lord it over' and 'exercise authority over' denote the use
of power and authority over others to one's own
advantage and their disadvantage; they convey the idea of
exploitation of the ruled by the ruler, the abuse of power
over other people's lives by those who possess it. This
observation of Jesus, suggesting as it does that the rulers
and the great ones of the Gentiles without exception

3

abuse their power, may perhaps at first strike us as rather too sweeping, as unduly pessimistic. But, when we reflect a little more, we can see that He was simply being realistic – with a proper biblical realism. For it is undoubtedly true that all who have worldly power are sinners and yield, some much more, some much less, but all of them to some extent, to the temptation to abuse their power, using it for selfish purposes, gratifying themselves at the expense of those over whom they wield it. How often do those who have power behave as though Providence – to use the vigorous language of Richard Rumbold's last speech before his execution – had 'sent a few men into the world ready booted and spurred to ride, and millions ready saddled and bridled to be ridden'![1] The only man possessed of power over the lives of others who has never yielded to the temptation to abuse it is our Lord Himself.

'But', Jesus goes on, 'it is not so among you.' This is an emphatic way of forbidding, a peremptory prohibition precluding all argument and debate. There is no room among the disciples of Jesus for this sort of thing, no room for any sort of lordliness which takes for granted the inferiority of others and one's right to their deference and service, no room for thinking in terms of superiority and precedence. In the Church of Christ, the fellowship of believers, the other person is never someone to be exploited, used for one's own aggrandisement, in however refined a way – and there are many subtle, and not immediately obvious, ways in which this can be done.

In the rest of verse 43 and in verse 44 Jesus gives the positive command which answers to the prohibition we have just been considering: 'but whosoever would become

[1] T. B. Macaulay, *The History of England from the Accession of James II*, Everyman's Library Edition, Vol. I, p. 433.

great among you, shall be your minister: and whosoever would be first among you, shall be servant of all.' Greatness in the Church consists in humble service of one's fellows. The word translated 'minister' is one which to the ears of pagan Greeks had an unpleasant sound: it suggested particularly the idea of lowly personal service rendered to another. The 'minister' is one whose energies are spent not in his own interest but in the interest of someone else. So leadership and pre-eminence in the Church consist in being at the service of the community for its true good. Or, to put it otherwise, importance in the Church is measured in terms of service, not of being served – by the extent to which one's life is directed not towards the benefit, advantage and advancement of oneself, but towards the benefit, advantage and advancement of others, by the extent to which one lives for others, one's life being not one's own but theirs (the word translated 'servant' here means properly 'slave').

But we have to confess that nowhere in the Church on earth is the pattern which our Lord here establishes as the only true pattern of responsibility and authority among His disciples fully realized. Instead the patterns of the world have to a very large extent been reproduced in the Church's life, sometimes quite blatantly and obviously and sometimes subtly and in ways which at first sight are not noticeable at all; and Christians everywhere tend to think of ecclesiastical responsibility and authority in terms of worldly power and worldly greatness.

But this is something which the Church, in so far as it is the Church of Jesus Christ, can never accept complacently. Nor will it give way to the temptation to pretend that the situation is other than it is, maintaining a comfortable blindness to the truth. Rather will it always be resisting the tendency to corruption within its life. Over it there stands continually the imperative: 'Be not fashioned according to this world: but be ye transformed by the renewing of your mind, that ye may prove what is the good and acceptable and perfect will of God' (Romans 12.2). With ever-renewed repentance for the extent of its conformity to the world it must seek again and again to open its life to Christ's criticism and instruction, so that the pattern which He has laid down for it may be more clearly exhibited in its life.

The last verse of this passage indicates the ground for the peremptory prohibition and the positive statement contained in verses 43 and 44: 'For verily the Son of man came not to be ministered unto, but to minister, and to give his life a ransom for many.' Jesus Christ did not come from the Father into this world, in order to be waited upon, to arrogate to Himself at all times as His inalienable right 'V.I.P.' service, to have a gay and comfortable and gracious time at the expense of men. On the contrary, He came 'in deep humility', in order to wait on men, to render, not to receive, service. 'For ye know the grace of our Lord Jesus Christ,' says St Paul, 'that, though he was rich, yet for your sakes he became poor, that ye through his poverty might become rich' (2 Corinthians 8.9).

Since this is so, since the Son of man Himself came to serve, not to be served, the disciple who looks for deference and service as his right, and expects a comfortable, gracious life at the expense of his fellow-men, is turning his back upon the gospel. All lordliness in the Church is a denial of the gospel. Such an attitude is out of order within the Church of Christ for the simple reason that it is inconsistent with the ministry of the Son of man.

And Jesus further indicates what is the climax of the Son of man's ministering. It is the giving of His life as a ransom for many. How else could He really adequately serve sinners? We are such that no service short of this could really meet our need. What this giving of His life as a ransom means and why it was necessary we shall see more clearly in the course of the following sermons. We may get a certain amount of light in the meantime on the significance of the word 'ransom' from a consideration of the various ways in which it is used in the Old Testament. It is used, for example, of the half-shekel poll-tax, 'a ransom for his soul unto the LORD', in Exodus 30.12; of the money a man had to pay to redeem his life which was forfeit because his ox had killed someone (Exodus 21.30); of the price paid for the redemption of the firstborn (Numbers 17.15); of the money by which the next of kin could ransom an enslaved relative (Leviticus 25.51–52); or of the payment for the redemption of a mortgaged property (Leviticus 25.26). More light is to be had from a consideration of Isaiah 52.13–53.12, which speaks of the suffering Servant of the Lord whose life is to be 'an offering for sin' (53.10). There is very little doubt (with all due respect to those who have recently argued to the contrary) that Jesus thought of Himself as fulfilling the prophecy of the Servant of the Lord who was to suffer vicariously for the sins of others; and it is extremely probable that we should discern in this verse echoes of Isaiah 53.10–12. But even Isaiah 52.13–53.12 does not provide us with a ready-made explanation of the whole significance of the cross of Christ. While we must accept every bit of light which the Old Testament has to offer us here, we must seek to discover the meaning of the Passion above all in the actual history which the Gospels relate. The Old Testament provides us with indispensable clues, and it is folly to ignore them; but we have always to remember that Jesus not only fulfils the Old Testament expectation but also transcends it.

7

One more point remains to be made here. Jesus speaks of the Son of man giving His life as a ransom – for many. Here John Calvin and Charles Wesley may stand side by side as witnesses to the same truth. In his exposition of this verse in his *Commentary on a Harmony of the Evangelists, Matthew, Mark, and Luke* John Calvin says: 'The word *many* . . . is not put definitely for a fixed number, but for a large number; for he contrasts himself with all others. And in this sense it is used in Romans 5.15, where Paul does not speak of any part of men, but embraces the whole human race.' Similarly in commenting on Mark 14.25 he says: 'By the word *many* he means not a part of the world only, but the whole human race.' Charles Wesley testifies to the same truth in these words:

> Father, whose everlasting love
>   Thy only Son for sinners gave,
> Whose grace to all did freely move,
>   And sent Him down the world to save:

> Help us Thy mercy to extol,
>   Immense, unfathomed, unconfined;
> To praise the Lamb who died for all,
>   The general Saviour of mankind.

> Thy undistinguishing regard
>   Was cast on Adam's fallen race;
> For all Thou hast in Christ prepared
>   Sufficient, sovereign, saving grace.

> The world He suffered to redeem;
>   For all He hath the atonement made;

For those that will not come to Him
The ransom of His life was paid. ...[1]

The use of 'many' in the sense of 'all' in this verse is a quite common Semitic idiom.

And since Christ's sufferings and death were for all men, since He gave His life as a ransom for the whole human race, there rests continually upon His people the obligation to bring the message of His cross to every man. The Church on earth can never be content so long as a single human being does not know that Christ died for him.

O Lord Jesus Christ, who camest not to be ministered unto but to minister and to give Thy life a ransom for many, forgive us, we beseech Thee, for all the ways in which we have increased the disorder of Thy Church by the conformity of our thoughts and lives to the patterns of worldly power and lordship. Fashion us anew after the pattern of Thy humility, that we may learn to serve one another gladly; and do Thou look mercifully upon all those who know not yet that Thy life was given for them; for Thy Name's sake. Amen.

[1] *The Methodist Hymn-Book*, hymn 75.

2

THE ENTRY INTO JERUSALEM

And when they draw nigh unto Jerusalem, unto Bethphage and Bethany, at the mount of Olives, he sendeth two of his disciples, and saith unto them, Go your way into the village that is over against you: and straightway as ye enter into it, ye shall find a colt tied, whereon no man ever yet sat; loose him, and bring him. And if any one say unto you, Why do ye this, say ye, The Lord hath need of him; and straightway he will send him back hither. And they went away, and found a colt tied at the door without in the open street; and they loose him. And certain of them that stood there said unto them, What do ye, loosing the colt? And they said unto them even as Jesus had said: and they let them go. And they bring the colt unto Jesus, and cast on him their garments; and he sat upon him. And many spread their garments upon the way; and others branches, which they had cut from the fields. And they that went before, and they that followed, cried, Hosanna; Blessed *is* he that cometh in the name of the Lord: Blessed *is* the kingdom that cometh, *the kingdom* of our father David: Hosanna in the highest.

And he entered into Jerusalem, into the temple; and when he had looked round about upon all things, it being now eventide, he went out unto Bethany with the twelve.

(Mark 11.1–11.)

There is no doubt that Mark, when he wrote this passage,

recognized that what he was relating was the entry of the true King of Israel, the Lord's Messiah, into His capital city. He saw in the riding on the colt the fulfilment of Zechariah 9.9: 'Rejoice greatly, O daughter of Zion . . .: behold, thy king cometh unto thee: he is just, and having salvation; lowly, and riding upon an ass, even upon a colt the foal of an ass.' He probably also saw in the spreading of the garments an act of royal homage to the King of Israel like that with which Jehu's fellow-officers had done homage to him when they learned what had been the message which the man of God had brought him. We read in 2 Kings 9.13 how 'they hasted, and took every man his garment, and put it under him on the top of the stairs, and blew the trumpet, saying, Jehu is king'.

But what about the actual incident itself? How far was its royal – its messianic – significance recognized at the time? It is often taken for granted that Jesus was by His action of riding on the colt claiming quite openly to be the Messiah and so deliberately challenging the nation. And the spreading of the garments and branches and the shouting are often interpreted as a consciously messianic demonstration on the part of His followers and the crowd. But this interpretation is for a number of reasons most unlikely. For one thing, it is highly significant that Mark, though he himself was conscious of the inner meaning of the incident he was relating, has refrained from suggesting, at any rate at all obviously, that this meaning was recognized at the time by the crowd of pilgrims or by the disciples. There is, in fact, when one looks at Mark's narrative more closely, a striking restraint. It is noteworthy also that there is no trace in the Gospels of this incident's having been mentioned at the trial before Pontius Pilate: but, had it been the sort of thing that it is often assumed to have been, the Jewish leaders would surely have made use of it, for it would have provided just the kind of evidence they needed. Indeed, had the incident been anything like a consciously messianic demonstration by supporters of Jesus, the Romans would surely have arrested Him at once and not waited for the Jewish authorities to take the initiative; for at Passover time they were always on the watch for trouble and ready to deal promptly and decisively with anything which looked as if it might lead to a disturbance. Moreover, there is a most significant verse in St John's account of this episode. In John 12.16 we read: 'These things understood not his disciples at the first: but when Jesus was glorified, then remembered they that these things were written of him, and that they had done these things unto him.' The Fourth Evangelist here seems to be reproducing an early and reliable tradition, according to which even the disciples did not understand at the time the significance of what was happening, but only came to see what it all meant and to realize the connection between Jesus' riding on the colt and the messianic prophecy of Zechariah after the Resurrection. If this is true, if the disciples did not at the time understand the messianic significance of what was happening, it is most unlikely that those who were not close followers of Jesus understood it.

The right conclusion to draw would seem to be that our Lord's borrowing the colt and riding it into the city was not an open claim to Messiahship, and that neither the crowd nor the disciples were conscious of the messianic meaning of His action. The spreading of the garments and foliage was probably quite a small affair, a spontaneous expression of respect for the prophet of Nazareth; while what is related in verse 9 ('And they that went before, and they that followed, cried, Hosanna; Blessed is he that cometh in the name of the Lord') need in no way imply any realization that Jesus was the messianic King. The words are from Psalm 118, one of the Psalms which were sung at the Passover. For pilgrims going up to the Passover to start singing it would perhaps be no more surprising than for a company of Christians at Christmas time to take up a carol. It could even be that the sight of the foliage being strewn in the way reminded someone of the bundles of foliage which in the Feast of Tabernacles were waved at the occurrence in the liturgy of the word 'Hosanna' and for this reason were sometimes referred to as 'hosannas'. And the patriotic words of verse 10 were natural enough in view of the associations of the festival, which was always the occasion of patriotic feeling. There is no need to assume that those who used them were thinking of Jesus as the Messiah.

We have still to ask about Jesus' own intention. It is clear that He took the initiative in the matter of the colt, and it is hardly open to doubt that He Himself intended to fulfil the words of Zechariah 9.9. But He probably also realized that the circumstances were such as to make it unlikely that the meaning of His action would be recognized at the time. It seems that He deliberately fulfilled the prophecy, in order that His disciples, while they would not be likely to see the significance of the sign at the time, might recognize it afterwards, and know that the prophetic word had been fulfilled. It would then serve to confirm for them the truth of His messiahship. If this interpretation of the narrative is correct, the entry of Jesus into Jerusalem on the first Palm Sunday was of a piece with the rest of His ministry. On this occasion, as throughout the rest of His ministry (except for the Transfiguration), His glory was veiled. This King who rode into Jerusalem on Palm Sunday was indeed a paradoxical King, a 'poor beggar-king' – to use Luther's phrase – riding a borrowed beast, and that an untrained colt with an improvised saddle of borrowed clothing. And the acclamations and attentions of His followers were so insignificant that neither the Jewish nor the Roman authorities even noticed them.

What then has this passage to say to us? What is its message? In the first place, it points us to Jesus of Nazareth as the true King of Israel, the Messiah promised by God to His people, and by them long expected. The moment of His entry into Jerusalem was the moment up to which all Israel's history had been leading. At last He had come, the true Son of David, to David's city. But He did not look like a king – on His borrowed ass. So, too, today He cannot be recognized except by faith. He does not prove His kingship to us by spectacular proofs. He does not compel us to believe. He leaves us free to make our own decision. Not till His final coming will the veiledness be done away, and His glory be made manifest to all. The question for us is: Will we recognize in this Rider on the borrowed ass our King? The testimony of Scripture is this, that, for those who receive Him as their King, He brings great joy. 'Rejoice greatly, . . . thy king cometh unto thee: he is just, and having salvation; lowly, and riding upon an ass, even upon a colt the foal of an ass' (Zechariah 9.9). The message of Palm Sunday is a summons to joy.

In the second place, this passage reminds us forcibly that our Lord Jesus is indeed the Messiah of *Israel*, the King of the *Jews*. And this is something which we Gentile Christians need to remember. For even in its unbelief the Jewish nation is still the people into whose bosom He was born as man, among whom He lived on earth, of whose blood He is, whose King He still is. And we cannot have the Jew Jesus as our Saviour, and at the same time be unwilling to have His people as our brothers and sisters. Antisemitism is always a denial of Jesus Christ.

In the third place, this passage sets before us the divinely-appointed pattern for the Church's life. The collect for the Sunday next before Easter in the Book of Common Prayer speaks very appropriately of 'the example of his great humility' and of God's purpose that 'all mankind' should follow it. But again and again the Church has been unwilling to tread in its King's footsteps. Again and again it has preferred to seek to impress men by its power, its worldly and altogether obvious power, its wealth, its costly and magnificent buildings, its pomp and splendour, and the support of the mighty of the earth, instead of seeking to win them by the power of the gospel and by self-forgetting love and humble unostentatious service. And now in the age of the television camera and the public-relations experts, the old temptations have become all the more seductive, and the danger of the various denominations' despising the example of the Lord's humility has been vastly increased.

But the lure of the appeal to outward success and impressiveness is not only a continual danger for the Church as a whole; it also haunts the pathway of the individual Christian. On the one hand, we are tempted to depend on the wrong things, to hanker after the gratitude and admiration of men and inordinately to desire superficial success, and, when success comes our way, to rely upon its appeal, instead of realizing that the hallmark of discipleship is not the applause of men, but steadfast obedience to Christ and the humble self-forgetting love which serves men, not for the sake of their esteem, but in order to express gratitude to Jesus Christ. And on the other hand, when we have to suffer the hardship, so

15

difficult to endure, of not being in a position to appeal to obvious success or outward impressiveness, we are tempted to lose heart. The narrative we have been considering calls us to follow the example of Christ's humility, and not to be surprised or discouraged, when the evidence of success and impressiveness seems all to be on the side of our adversaries, and obedience to Christ to bring nothing but frustration and apparent failure, but to remember how on the first Palm Sunday, while all the trappings of power and authority and prestige were with Pilate and Annas and Caiaphas, the Son of God had only a borrowed ass and makeshift saddle.

Almighty and everlasting God, who, of thy tender love towards mankind, hast sent thy Son, our Saviour Jesus Christ, to take upon him our flesh, and to suffer death upon the cross, that all mankind should follow the example of his great humility: Mercifully grant, that we may both follow the example of his patience, and also be made partakers of his resurrection; through the same Jesus Christ our Lord. Amen. (Collect for the Sunday next before Easter.)

3

THE CLEANSING OF THE TEMPLE

And they come to Jerusalem: and he entered into the
temple, and began to cast out them that sold and
them that bought in the temple, and overthrew the
tables of the money-changers, and the seats of them
that sold the doves; and he would not suffer that any
man should carry a vessel through the temple. And
he taught, and said unto them, Is it not written, My
house shall be called a house of prayer for all the
nations? but ye have made it a den of robbers. And
the chief priests and the scribes heard it, and sought
how they might destroy him: for they feared him, for
all the multitude was astonished at his teaching.

(Mark 11.15–18.)

After entering Jerusalem on Palm Sunday Jesus went into
the Temple, and, 'when he had looked round about upon
all things', as it was evening, He went back again – so
Mark tells us – over the Mount of Olives to Bethany. The
next day He and the Twelve returned to the city, and once
again entered the Temple. This time He 'began to cast out
them that sold and them that bought in the temple, and
overthrew the tables of the money-changers, and the seats
of them that sold the doves'.

The mart was there for the convenience of pilgrims. It
was naturally more convenient to be able to buy on the
spot the animals (John mentions oxen and sheep as well as
doves) and other requirements for sacrifices than to have
to bring them from home; there was, besides, the big
advantage that the animals sold in the Temple precincts

17

had already been certified as suitable for sacrifice, whereas animals brought from home would be subject to official inspection and might in the end be rejected as blemished and unsuitable. The case for the money-changing was similar. The Temple dues had to be paid in the Tyrian coinage, the Tyrian shekel being the nearest thing available to the old Hebrew shekel. So it was necessary for pilgrims to be able to change their ordinary currency. The mart and the money-changing, as well as being a convenience for pilgrims, were, no doubt, also an extremely lucrative business for those concerned in them. All this business seems to have taken place in the Court of the Gentiles. The explanation of the further detail given in verse 16 ('and he would not suffer that any man should carry a vessel through the temple') is probably that Jesus was seeking to give effect to an existing prohibition which had been allowed to become a dead letter. In the Jewish Mishnah it is said that a man 'may not enter the Temple Mount with his staff or his sandal or his wallet, or with the dust upon his feet, nor may he make of it a short by-path . . . .'.

Jesus did not merely act, and act with resolution and decisiveness: He went on to state the grounds of His action. 'And he taught, and said unto them, Is it not written, My house shall be called a house of prayer for all the nations? but ye have made it a den of robbers.' The first part of Jesus' words, as recorded here, is an appeal to Isaiah 56.7. According to God's Word the Temple was to be 'an house of prayer for all peoples'; but there was only one area of the Temple which non-Jews were allowed to enter, namely, the Court of the Gentiles. A stone barrier (which Paul no doubt had in mind when he referred to 'the middle wall of partition' in Ephesians 2.14) used to separate this area from the rest of the Temple, and there still exists a pillar from it bearing the following inscription: 'No foreigner is permitted to enter within the barrier and enclosure round the Temple. Whoever is caught doing so will have himself to blame that his death ensues.' But the mart in the Court of the Gentiles was effectively preventing the one place in the Temple where the Gentiles were allowed from being a place of prayer. Thus under pretence of facilitating the true worship of God, men were thwarting His purpose for His Temple. The second part of what Jesus said is reminiscent of Jeremiah 7.11, which is part of Jeremiah's famous sermon at the gate of the Temple. Jesus was doubtless referring to the swindling which was going on. It was easy to fleece the pilgrims who had to have the wherewithal, if they were going to fulfil the purpose of their pilgrimage. He was possibly also thinking that, even apart from such swindling, the whole business was, in a deeper sense, a robbery – a robbing God of the honour due to His Name, as well as a robbing the Gentiles of their place of prayer.

The inner, hidden, significance of Jesus' action was indeed messianic, and more than messianic. To quote Calvin's comment, 'He declared Himself to be both King and High Priest, who presided over the Temple and the worship of God.' The true Messiah had at last come to God's holy Temple, the very Son of God to His own Father's house, God Himself to the place which He had chosen 'to cause His name to dwell there'. The prophecy of Malachi 3.1–2 was being fulfilled: '. . . the Lord, whom ye seek, shall suddenly come to his temple . . . But who may abide the day of his coming, and who shall stand when he appeareth?' But outwardly Jesus' action, while it may well have caused the chief priests and scribes to think, did not go beyond the assertion of a prophet's authority. Its messianic, and more than messianic, meaning was veiled. Had there been anything at all openly messianic about it, the Romans would surely have acted at once.

But He who at the end of His earthly ministry came to the Temple in Jerusalem, comes now as the exalted Lord again and again to His Church in Scripture and Sacrament, to assert His lordship over us and to claim our obedience. He comes in mercy and in judgment, to reveal to us the disorder of our life, of the life of the Church and of our individual lives, and to recall us to order. And the question which this passage puts to us is: Are we going to be like the chief priests and the scribes and resent His interference, or are we going to welcome Him as the Lord to whom we belong and let Him have free course with us, opening our hearts and lives to His criticism and correction? To put it otherwise, are we prepared to be engaged in conversation by Him, and not to break off the conversation when it becomes uncomfortable? Are we prepared to wrestle with Scripture, to study it diligently and persistently? – for it is through the Bible that He wishes to speak to us, taking the words of Scripture and making them again and again the vehicle of His conversation with us. This is for us all an urgent question, the question of the Church's health or sickness. For churches which call themselves Reformed it is peculiarly sobering; for the Church is healthy in so far as it is continually being held in conversation by Christ, continually held open to His criticism and correction, His mercy and forgiveness and renewing power; and it is truly Reformed, not merely as having once been reformed more than four centuries ago, but in so far as it is continually being reformed by its King and Head.

But let us look a bit more closely at this passage; for, while, as we have seen, it reminds us quite generally of

Christ's right to lay His finger upon everything in our lives which is contrary to His will, and questions us generally about our readiness to be called to order by Him, it also puts to us some rather more specific questions.

When Jesus charged His hearers with having made the Temple of God 'a den of robbers', He no doubt had in mind the extortion and swindling which had been going on in the Temple court. Through this passage Christian congregations are questioned by Christ about the fairness and honesty of their own dealings. Are they always such as bring honour to the Church of Christ? Or do Christian congregations sometimes drive hard bargains? Does a congregation which pays its pastor a minimum stipend ever do even that grudgingly, and then think it has bought him body and soul, day and night, week in week out, and his wife into the bargain? Are church-officers always treated with fairness and generosity? And do we always remember that the money which has been solemnly dedicated to God in our Sunday worship is no longer ours to dispose of according to our human whims and fancies, and that the congregation which uses such money otherwise than with a proper sense of responsibility to Christ is guilty of sacrilege, of the misappropriation of a holy thing? Do we, who are the spiritual heirs of John Calvin, always remember the truth which he so vigorously emphasized, that the possessions of the Church are the patrimony of the poor? Or do we, at a time when two thirds of the world's population are hungry, squander on unnecessary prestige projects and amenities designed for our own comfort that which by right belongs to Christ in His needy brethren?

Jesus also quoted Isaiah 56.7. God had purposed that His Temple should be 'a house of prayer for all the nations', but the Jews were holding a market in the Court of the Gentiles – in the only place in the Temple which non-Jews were allowed to enter. And God has purposed that His Church should be 'a house of prayer for all the nations', the means by which they should come to the knowledge of Christ their Saviour, a refuge and home for all men. Certainly our congregations have supported for many years a vast missionary endeavour with much generosity and often with real self-sacrifice. But have we not also often seriously hindered the Church's missionary work, and sometimes stultified it, by our compromises with the evils of colonialism, and by our failure to speak out courageously and firmly and unambiguously against injustice and oppression?

And, nearer home, what sort of welcome do we give in our churches to overseas students, West Indian and other immigrants, and other strangers who may need our friendship? And is the life of our congregations turned outward in evangelism and practical service, and in responsibility for the communities in which it is set? Or are our churches too often turned in upon themselves, resembling clubs and cliques, rather than congregations of the Church of Jesus Christ, existing largely for themselves, for their own welfare and edification and sometimes even for little more than their own entertainment? How real has been our concern for the unchurched masses, for the bewildered and aimless young people, for the misfits and outcasts of society, for the dossers, for the inmates of our prisons, and for discharged prisoners? Must we not confess that very often and in various ways we have, by our lack of vision and lack of imagination and lack of sensitiveness to the needs of others, and by the pettiness and self-centredness of much of our churchmanship, made it more difficult for those outside to find in the Church 'a house of prayer for all the nations' – more difficult for them to find their way to Christ their Saviour?

Thus in this passage the Lord Jesus Christ puts to us searching and uncomfortable questions, and disturbs our peace of mind. What is our reaction going to be? The chief priests and the scribes resented Jesus' actions and words, 'and sought how they might destroy him', the disturber of their peace, the questioner of the things they took for granted. Are we too going to resent His interference in our lives and in the life of our churches, and to try to ignore it or cover it over as best we can? Or are we going to hold ourselves open to Him and let Him hold us in conversation and assert His lordship over our lives?

O Lord Jesus Christ, who through the words of Scripture and in the power of the Holy Spirit comest to us Thy people in mercy and judgment, as once Thou didst come to the Temple in Jerusalem, we confess before Thee, that we have filled Thy Church with our sins. By our selfishness and our blindness we have closed the Kingdom of God against men, and caused Thy Name to be blasphemed. Assert Thy authority over us, we beseech Thee; make us to recognize our sins and grant that we may submit ourselves to Thee, who art our Saviour and Lord; for Thy Name's sake. Amen.

4

THE INSTITUTION OF THE HOLY SUPPER

For I received of the Lord that which also I delivered
unto you, how that the Lord Jesus in the night in
which he was betrayed took bread; and when he had
given thanks, he brake it, and said, This is my body,
which is for you: this do in remembrance of me. In
like manner also the cup, after supper, saying, This
cup is the new covenant in my blood: this do, as oft
as ye drink *it*, in remembrance of me. For as often as
ye eat this bread, and drink the cup, ye proclaim the
Lord's death till he come.

(1 Corinthians 11. 23–26.)

There is no doubt that this is our earliest written account
of the Last Supper; for 1 Corinthians was written at least a
decade before the earliest of our Gospels, that of Mark.
Even if the contention of some scholars that Mark 14
actually preserves an earlier form of the tradition than
that which is given here should prove to be correct, 1
Corinthians 11.23–26 would still, as the earliest written
account, be of immense value. And we owe it to the
disorders at the celebrations of the Eucharist in Corinth!
It was – so verses 17–22 make clear – the information that
Paul had received about these which was the occasion for
his discussing the subject.

I

These verses tell us first of all *what Jesus did at the Last*

Supper. They tell us that He acted as the head of the house in a Jewish meal – it was probably the Passover meal – in the company of His disciples. He followed the ordinary Jewish customs, but He gave at certain points a new significance to them. (The primitive tradition which Paul is here passing on did not mention all the details of the meal, but concentrated only on those features which were continued in the Christian Eucharist, the points at which Jesus gave new meaning to the age-old customs.) In so doing, Jesus did three things.

(i) He interpreted for His disciples His approaching death. This He had already tried to do on a number of occasions, particularly in the three predictions of the Passion (Mark 8.31; 9.31; 10.32–34), and in the 'ransom' saying (Mark 10.45). But it is clear that the disciples were very slow to comprehend. So now once more He interpreted to them the meaning of what was about to happen, in order that at any rate after the event they might be able to look back and understand. This comes out most clearly in the words about the wine, 'This cup is the new covenant in my blood.' Jesus was indicating that the shedding of His blood was to be the ratification of the new covenant prophesied by Jeremiah (Jeremiah 31.31ff). As the Old Covenant had been ratified by the sprinkling of the sacrificial blood (Exodus 24.6–8), so God's New Covenant with men was about to be established by Jesus' death; and, as being sprinkled with the sacrificial blood by Moses had made the Israelites partakers in the Old Covenant, so those who shared the cup of wine were being made partakers in the benefits and obligations of the New Covenant. Thus Jesus stamped a sacrificial significance upon His approaching death. It was to be the sacrificial means to a new relationship of men to God.

(ii) He instituted a new rite for His disciples. This is the significance of the words, 'this do in remembrance of me', 'this do, as oft as ye drink it, in remembrance of me'. He commanded His disciples to repeat His significant actions. Hence the words in the Prayer of Consecration in the Order of the Administration of the Lord's Supper in the Book of Common Prayer: '. . . and did institute, and in his holy Gospel command us to continue, a perpetual memory of that his precious death, until his coming again . . .'

(iii) He gave to his disciples, as He was about to be parted from them, the pledge and means of His real personal presence with them, though unseen, in the days between His departure from them and His coming again. He realized that it was the last time that He would have this meal with them in the conditions of His earthly life. They were about to enter the time of separation, the time between the present supper and the final reunion. During that interval they would again and again eat together, but without Him. So he appointed for them a token and pledge of His presence with them during the days of separation. The bread broken and distributed in the familiar way was to have a new significance: henceforth it was to be both the pledge and the means of His real, though unseen, personal presence in their midst. Their repetition of the meal would be the trysting-time and -place, His appointed tryst with His disciples.

II

In the second place, these verses tell us *what the exalted Lord of the Church does in the Holy Supper*.

(i) He keeps His tryst with His Church, and comes to us unseen yet personally and really. He gives Himself, His real presence, to us. This is the primary gift of the Holy Supper. But let us never forget that He comes to us as the Lord – not conjured up by us, not dispensed by some magic at our disposal, but in His freedom and faithfulness, through the Holy Spirit. So the early Church prayed *Marana tha* ('Our Lord, come') in its liturgy, looking both to His final coming and to His intermediate unseen comings, and expecting Him in the Supper being celebrated. That is why the Supper is closely connected with Easter, even more closely than with Good Friday – in fact, Good Friday is the one day in the year on which traditionally the Supper is not celebrated! – for it looks back to the meals which the risen Lord had with His disciples, as well as to the Last Supper. That is why Sunday, the Lord's Day, the day of His resurrection, is, above all the days of the week, the day for its celebration; and in its celebration the note of joy should always be prominent. And one of the most appropriate hymns for Communion is the great French hymn, *A toi la gloire, O Ressuscité* ('Thine be the glory, risen, conquering Son'), which contains the verse:

'Lo! Jesus meets us, risen from the tomb;
Lovingly He greets us, scatters fear and gloom;
Let the Church with gladness, hymns of triumph sing,
For her Lord now liveth, death hath lost its sting.'[1]

(ii) He feeds us with His body and blood, and makes us sharers in the benefits of His passion, the benefits and obligations of the New Covenant established by His

[1] E. L. Budry, translated by R. B. Hoyle. *The Methodist Hymn-Book*, hymn 213.

27

death. As Melchizedek brought forth bread and wine for Abraham (Genesis 14.18),

'Behold, the eternal King and Priest
Brings forth for me the bread and wine.'[1]

He is here the host and the banquet at the same time.

III

In the third place, these verses tell us *what we do in the Holy Supper*. Note that it is, of course, Christ's action in the Supper which is primary and fundamental. What we do is only secondary, a response to what He does. But precisely because what we do is response to His prior and more important action, it too is of very great importance.

(i) We obey Christ. We do what we do in obedience to Him. It is He who appointed the Sacrament, and said, 'This do in remembrance of me', 'This do, as oft as ye drink it, in remembrance of me.' Our action is response to His command. He, of course, commands many hard things, which we can only obey very imperfectly and inadequately and feebly. But this is easy – so easy that we can all obey it. It is therefore a specially clear test of our desire to obey Him.

There is something extraordinarily salutary in thus doing the simple thing He bids us, simply because He bids us do it. It may be that we do not feel that we get much benefit from the Sacrament. But, whether we are conscious of being benefited or not, we ought to do this, because He has commanded it. That is a sufficient, the all-

[1] Anonymous. *Congregational Praise*, hymn 307.

sufficient, reason. And, if we faithfully continue to do it out of obedience to Christ, we shall surely at some time come to benefit consciously too.

(ii) We receive. In the Supper we receive bread and eat it, we receive wine and drink it. This is of course presupposed by the verses which we are considering. What is the meaning of this receiving of bread and wine?

As we receive the bread and wine, we receive Jesus Christ Himself, who keeps His promise to be with us (Matthew 28.20), His promise in the institution of the Supper ('This is my body'). Our receiving Him is the correlative of His presence, of His gift of Himself, the response to His action. In the Supper we expect Him, and as He comes to us, we greet Him.

As we receive the bread and wine, we receive Him as the food and drink of our souls, and give our souls to Him to be fed, and are made partakers in all the benefits of His passion. We cannot explain how He feeds us, but we receive in faith, believing His promises. 'Now, if anyone should ask me how this takes place,' says Calvin, 'I shall not be ashamed to confess that it is a secret too lofty for either my mind to comprehend or my words declare. And, to speak more plainly, I rather experience than understand it. Therefore, I here embrace without controversy the truth of God in which I may safely rest. He declares his flesh the food of my soul, his blood its drink. I offer my soul to him to be fed with such food. In his Sacred Supper he bids me take, eat, and drink his body and blood under the symbols of bread and wine. I do not doubt that he himself truly presents them, and that I receive them.'[1] And feeding on Him thus through the

---

[1] *Institutes of the Christian Religion*, IV.xvii.32 (quoted according to the translation of F. L. Battles, London, 1961).

means of bread and wine, we are directed to look upward to where He is at the right hand of God.

By receiving the bread and wine, we acknowledge our need. As we take and eat, take and drink, we acknowledge our deep hunger and thirst, our emptiness, poverty and sin. We are empty and need to be satisfied with true food and drink, we are sinners and need to be forgiven and cleansed.

By receiving the bread and wine, we accept Him as the One who has the right to dispose of our lives, to lay His commands upon us as our Lord. By receiving we re-dedicate ourselves to Him, to His service (and therefore also to the service of our neighbours). We take upon ourselves the obligations of the New Covenant.

(iii) We remember Him. According to St Paul Jesus used the words, 'this do in remembrance of me' and 'this do, as oft as ye drink it, in remembrance of me'. As the Jews in the Passover remember (and in a real sense relive) the event of God's deliverance of the children of Israel from Egyptian bondage, so Christians in the Holy Supper remember the event of their redemption, their deliverance, the historic deed of God in the life of poverty and hardship, the humiliation, sufferings, death, resurrection and ascension of Jesus Christ. We should, of course, always remember this, always remember our Lord in His earthly life and ministry. 'Remember Jesus Christ . . .', says 2 Timothy 2.8. But here in the Supper we are given, and accept, and use, a special opportunity of remembering Him.

And here we are reminded that our faith rests on historic facts. It is rooted and grounded in what God has done in history, in real events. As we, in remembrance of Jesus, repeat the actions which He did at the Last Supper, we acknowledge this. This is something which is especially important at the present time, when some influential teachers seem to be intent on dissolving the saving events of the gospel into a mere existentialist philosophy. Not that remembering the historic Jesus is all! If the Supper were only a memorial, we should indeed be poor. But it certainly is a memorial. As we receive the living, exalted Lord through the work of the Holy Spirit and by means of the elements of bread and wine, and, so receiving Him present, look up in faith to where He is at God's right hand, we also look back to His historic life and death and resurrection and ascension. For the living Lord whom we worship with the Father and the Holy Spirit is the same Jesus Christ who once died for us and was raised from the dead by the power of the Father.

And remembering His earthly ministry, His sufferings, death, resurrection and ascension, we cannot help but give thanks to God. The Holy Supper is indeed a eucharist, a thanksgiving.

(iv) We proclaim, show forth, His death. Verse 26 is Paul's comment – 'For as often as ye eat this bread, and drink the cup, ye proclaim the Lord's death . . .' As often as Christians gather to celebrate the Holy Supper of their Lord, they take their place beside the apostles in proclaiming to the whole world the Cross of Jesus Christ as God's judgment, and God's redemption, of the world. What the congregation does in quiet privacy and intimacy is full of significance for the world outside; and this proclamation is, of course, also a proclamation to the Church – to one another. The fact that Christians again and again take bread and wine is well known to the world, and is – if only it would recognize it – a proclamation of that which is both the real judgment and also the real hope and promise of its life.

(v) We look forward to His final coming. 'For as often

as ye eat this bread, and drink the cup, ye proclaim the Lord's death till he come.' So alongside the looking upward and looking backward there is in the celebration of the Supper a looking forward. Our meeting with Christ in the Supper, our receiving Him, His real personal presence, though unseen, in the Sacrament, is the pledge of the final reunion with Him, when He shall come again in glory. This earthly feast, again and again shared, is the pledge and the foretaste of the marriage feast of the Lamb. We take our stand under the sign of hope. We allow our gaze, which is so often and so easily distracted from its proper Object, to be directed back toward our coming Lord. We allow ourselves to be reminded that it is our task – if we understand it properly according to the New Testament, our whole task! – to watch for Him, and so to be ever engaged the more earnestly in the work He has given us to do, striving to witness to Him, to proclaim His gospel to all men, and recognizing Him thankfully and joyfully in His intermediate comings in the persons of the least of His brethren.

My God, and is Thy table spread?
And does Thy cup with love o'erflow?
Thither be all Thy children led,
And let them all Thy sweetness know.

Hail, sacred feast, which Jesus makes,
Rich banquet of His flesh and blood!
Thrice happy he who here partakes
That Sacred Stream, that heavenly food!

Let crowds approach with hearts prepared;
With hearts inflamed let all attend,
Nor, when we leave our Father's board,
The pleasure or the profit end.

THE INSTITUTION OF THE HOLY SUPPER

O let Thy table honoured be,
And furnished well with joyful guests;
And may each soul salvation see
That here its sacred pledges tastes.
                                    Amen.

(Philip Doddridge. *The Church Hymnary*, 2nd ed., hymn 311).

5

GOOD FRIDAY

*. . . the blood of sprinkling that speaketh better than
that of Abel.*

(Hebrews 12.24.)

A Christian congregation does not gather together in
church on Good Friday to mourn, but to hear again the
glad tidings of the sufferings and death of Jesus Christ and
to celebrate God's mighty act for the redemption of the
world. The message of the Cross is glad tidings; for the
crucifixion has a sequel, and as Christians we cannot
think of the Cross except in the light of that sequel, the
resurrection and ascension of the Crucified. The words of
this text underline the word 'glad' in 'glad tidings',
because they indicate that in the cross of Jesus God has
really dealt with our real situation. We do not have to try
to forget our cares and anxieties and sins, when we gather
to worship God. Rather, we come before Him as the men
and women that we actually are, in our sinfulness and our
troubles, our sorrows and our fears, to hear His message
to our condition. His message is addressed to us just as we
are, and just where we are.

The context of these words is a paragraph concerned
with the Christian's access to God. In the course of it this
contrast is made between the effects of the death of Christ
and the effects of the death of Abel.

In the first place, we have to ask what the writer means
by 'the blood of Abel'. He is referring, of course, to the
story of Cain's murder of his brother Abel, which in the
first book of the Bible is the immediate sequel of the story

of the Fall, of man's rebellion against God's commandment, the close proximity of the two narratives no doubt being intended to suggest the truth that man's rebellion against God brings with it the destruction of brotherly relations between men. The story of Cain and Abel is a dramatic picture of human relations in this fallen world.

A far too pessimistic picture? That hateful things have been done, and still are being done, in many parts of the world in the mid-twentieth century, we would no doubt all of us willingly admit. We may think of the Nazis' attempt to exterminate the Jews of Europe, the terrible brutalities of the Algerian War, the hateful and senseless murders since the peace, the massacres of Sharpeville and Langa, and the suppression of the Hungarian people by Russian might. But all these things have been done by foreigners; it would surely be going too far to suggest that British churchgoers also come under the condemnation of Genesis 4! But would it?

Can we dissociate ourselves altogether from the South African Government's crimes against the black people of South Africa, so long as our own Government continues to supply arms to Dr Verwoerd in the full knowledge that they are likely to be used against the African population (as British Saracen armoured cars were in the Sharpeville massacre), and so long as Britain's vast financial stake in South Africa, rather than considerations of justice and humanity, continues to determine British policy with regard to South Africa? And can we forget that it was not the atheistic Communists of Russia or China, but the United States of America, the leader of the Western so-called Christian nations, which has the shameful distinction of being the first, and so far the only, power to use nuclear bombs in war? Can we forget Hiroshima and

Nagasaki? And do we forget so easily the Egyptians who lost their lives as a result of the British and French aggression against Egypt in 1956?

To come yet nearer home – there is the daily human sacrifice offered on our British roads to the idols of selfishness and thoughtlessness. And there is the fratricide of which we all are guilty inasmuch as we fail to save the lives which we in our affluence could so easily save – for the sixth commandment not only forbids actual murder, but also requires us to love our brother man and to do all in our power to prevent his hurt; and, as Calvin wrote, 'There is little difference between manslaughter and the conduct of him who does not concern himself about relieving a person in distress.' In this connection it is relevant to note that, as Dr R. Passmore of Edinburgh University has recently pointed out,[1] the evidence suggests that every four people in the prosperous parts of the world waste food enough to satisfy one inhabitant of an underdeveloped country. And does not the condemnation of Cain fall even on our Church life when we indulge, at a time when millions are starving, in needless extravagance in the decoration and equipment of our churches? Our newspapers lately carried reports of the placing of a solid silver cross costing about five thousand pounds on a cathedral altar; and how often – on a smaller scale, but with the same forgetfulness of our starving brothers – do our Free Church congregations do the same sort of thing! (To appeal to the altogether unique circumstances of the incident related in Mark 14.3–9 in defence of such heartlessness would, of course, be quite beside the point.)

And if we resent the suggestion that the story of Cain

[1] As reported in *The Guardian* of 7 April 1962, p. 3.

and Abel concerns our life, if we give way to the temptation to deny our responsibility, do we not then make all the clearer our likeness to Cain who replied to God's question, 'Where is thy brother Abel?' with the cynical words, 'I know not. Am I my brother's keeper?' But not only does each one of us play the part of Cain; we also all of us play – though unwillingly – the part of Abel. We not only hurt our brothers; we also suffer at our brothers' hands. Hurting and being hurt, wronging and being wronged, each of us plays a double role.

And, according to our text, the blood of Abel 'speaketh'. The writer to the Hebrews refers, of course, to Genesis 4.10–12: 'And he [that is, God] said, What hast thou done? the voice of thy brother's blood crieth unto me from the ground. And now cursed art thou from the ground, which hath opened her mouth to receive thy brother's blood from thy hand; when thou tillest the ground, it shall not henceforth yield unto thee her strength; a fugitive and a wanderer shalt thou be in the earth.' The blood of Abel cries out today. The sufferings inflicted on men by their fellows call for divine retribution upon those who have inflicted them. Moreover, God is not deaf. He hears the cry of Abel's blood, and He heeds it. Though He may seem to tarry, He is not mocked. Soon or late, we reap what we sow.

But the text refers to other blood that has been shed – 'the blood of sprinkling'. And it is about this other blood that we have, in the second place, to think. One came into our world, who, unlike all of us, never played the part of Cain. His hand was never against His brothers. Men slew Him like another Abel. But His death was not just like Abel's. He was not an unwilling victim. His death was voluntary. He laid down His life freely. Calvin speaks of His going to Gethsemane, to which He knew Judas would be coming, 'as if He had made an appointment with His enemies'. But more than this! He, who thus voluntarily 'presented Himself to death', was Jesus Christ, God's only Son as well as truly man. And so His death was God's mighty deed for the redemption of the world.

In His death He bore, not just men's hatred and spite, but the wrath of God against sin. So in Gethsemane He prayed, 'Abba, Father, all things are possible unto thee; remove this cup from me: howbeit not what I will, but what thou wilt' (Mark 14.36). In the Old Testament the word 'cup' is frequently used metaphorically with reference to the divine wrath, the divine punishment of sin. Thus, for example, in Isaiah 51.17–23 the prophet speaks of 'the cup of his [that is, God's] fury', 'the bowl of the cup of staggering', being taken away from Israel. In the Garden Jesus prayed that, if it were possible, the cup might be taken away from Him. But that could not be, if He was to obey His Father's will. Rather, He had to drink it to the dregs. Thus He 'bare the sin of many' (Isaiah 53.12), and 'the LORD hath laid on him the iniquity of us all' (Isaiah 53.6) and 'Him who knew no sin he [that is, God] made to be sin on our behalf' (2 Corinthians 5.21). In our place He bore the full consequences of our sin. The retribution, for which the blood of all the Abels of history cries out, fell on Him, the burden of the guilt of all the Cains.

We have just referred to the wrath of God. We must, of course, be careful not to misunderstand what the Bible means by this. We must remember that God's wrath is unlike ours, that it contains no element of vindictiveness, pettiness, or hypocrisy, but is the reaction to sin of Him who is altogether holy and righteous and loving. The expression is certainly one that can very easily be grievously misunderstood; but to try to explain the meaning of the Cross without taking into account the reality which it denotes would be to fail to take sin seriously and to misrepresent the gospel as shallow sentimentality.

Because Jesus Christ identified Himself with us to the uttermost and, in obedience to His Father's will and in faithfulness to us men, refused to let go of us, He endured to go down into those fearful depths of separation from God, which we have deserved as our portion, but which, because He has traversed them for us, we do not have to face. That is the meaning of the cry of dereliction, 'My God, my God, why hast thou forsaken me?' (Mark 15.34), words which we shall not want to water down or explain away, if we take God seriously and if we know something of the seriousness of sin (though we shall not deny, of course, that, even when Christ was enduring that abandonment on our behalf, the unity of the Blessed Trinity was in some way beyond our comprehension still unbroken). The cry of dereliction, by giving us a glimpse of the awful cost of our redemption, reveals to us both the true nature of sin, and, at the same time, the reality of our deliverance and the boundlessness of God's love.

In the third place, we have to ask what this text means when it says that Christ's blood 'speaketh better', or – to use the clearer translation of the Authorized Version – 'speaketh better things', than Abel's. We have already seen what Abel's blood speaks: it cries out everywhere for vengeance, for the punishment of man's inhumanity to man. What then are these 'better things' which Christ's blood speaks? We shall mention only some of them.

First, it speaks *God's forgiveness*. 'Christ died for our sins according to the scriptures', says St Paul (1 Corinthians 15.3). The testimony of the Bible is well summed up in the line of the hymn, 'He died that we might be forgiven'.[1] Through His death we have forgiveness. Though we have still to suffer some of the consequences of our sins, we do not have to bear the wrath of God; though as sinners we have still to die, death is not for us the fearful thing which it was for Jesus Christ. In the midst of the chaos of our sinning and being sinned against, God has given us in His forgiveness a firm ground upon which to take our stand. Day by day we may live as pardoned sinners; for 'There is . . . now no condemnation to them that are in Christ Jesus' (Romans 8.1). The load which we could never dislodge from our own shoulders has been removed and carried right away. But Christ's cry of dereliction on the cross makes it abundantly clear that this forgiveness is in no way a glossing over, condoning or belittling of our sin. The forgiveness which 'the blood of sprinkling' speaks is a forgiveness which is altogether worthy of the God who in all His ways is holy, righteous and true. There is therefore no unreality, no element of 'saying, Peace, peace; when there is no peace', about the healing and the liberation which it brings. And there is no question of any sin being so heinous as to be beyond the reach of this forgiveness; for in Christ's death the price of the sin of the whole world and of every single man was paid – in full. There is none who is not invited to come to Christ; and His promise stands: 'him that cometh to me I will in no wise cast out' (John 6.37).

Secondly, 'the blood of sprinkling' speaks *hope*. 'He that spared not his own Son, but delivered him up for us all, how shall he not also with him freely give us all things?' asks St Paul (Romans 8.32). The fact that God has taken upon Himself the burden of our sin, and

[1] *The Church Hymnary* (3rd ed.), hymn 241 ('There is a green hill far away').

40

reconciled us to Himself by the cross of Jesus Christ, forbids us to doubt either His will or His ability to save us finally and bring us to eternal life. We can be confident that He will *never* abandon those whom He has redeemed at such a cost. Even in a world menaced by the threat of nuclear war those who believe that 'God so loved the world, that he gave his only begotten Son' (John 3.16) are delivered from the bondage of fear and enabled to live in hope.

And, thirdly, 'the blood of sprinkling' speaks *the reconciliation of brethren.* By the Cross God has given us back our brother man as our brother, our 'brother for whose sake Christ died' (1 Corinthians 8.11). As such he cannot any longer be for us, who believe in Christ, one who in his weakness invites contempt and exploitation and in his strength fear and envy; he is henceforth the brother whom we may and must – and can – love and serve.

As we receive again the glad tidings of those 'better things' which Christ's blood speaks, we are summoned to set our whole lives once more under the sign of His cross and to re-dedicate ourselves to obedience to the Lord who died for us, joyfully taking our stand upon God's forgiveness, facing the future with confident hope, and recognizing gladly in our fellow-men the brothers for whose sake Christ died.

O Lord Jesus Christ, who didst suffer and die upon the cross for our redemption, we worship and adore Thee. Unto Thee, O Saviour of the world, be all honour and glory and thanksgiving for ever and ever. But Thou hast taught us where Thou wouldest be thanked. So grant that we who have this world's goods and behold our fellow-men in need, may not shut up our compassion from them, but, recognizing in each one of them Thy needy brother in whom Thou comest to claim our thanks and service, may love them not merely in word or with the tongue, but in deed and truth; to the honour of Thy blessed Name. Amen.

6

EASTER

And when the sabbath was past, Mary Magdalene,
and Mary the *mother* of James, and Salome, bought
spices, that they might come and anoint him. And
very early on the first day of the week, they came to
the tomb when the sun was risen. And they were
saying among themselves, Who shall roll us away
the stone from the door of the tomb? and looking up,
they see that the stone is rolled back: for it was
exceeding great. And entering into the tomb, they
saw a young man sitting on the right side, arrayed in
a white robe; and they were amazed. And he saith
unto them, Be not amazed: ye seek Jesus, the
Nazarene, which hath been crucified: he is risen; he is
not here: behold, the place where they laid him! But
go, tell his disciples and Peter, He goeth before you
into Galilee: there shall ye see him, as he said unto
you. And they went out, and fled from the tomb; for
trembling and astonishment had come upon them:
and they said nothing to any one; for they were
afraid.

(Mark 16.1–8.)

The first verse gives the names of the three persons whose
visit to the tomb of Jesus and whose experience there this
passage relates. 'Mary Magdalene, and Mary the mother
of James, and Salome' – they are all women. All four
Gospels make it clear that the first friends of Jesus to hear
the news of His resurrection were women. This is highly
significant; for the ancient Jews certainly did not have a

romantic attitude to women, nor did they consider them as on an equality with men. 'Sooner let the words of the Law be burnt than delivered to women'; 'Happy is he whose children are male, and alas for him whose children are female' – these quotations from the Talmud indicate the ancient Jewish attitude to women. And in the Morning Service in the Daily Prayer Book used by Jewish congregations in the British Commonwealth the men still say, 'Blessed art thou, O Lord our God, King of the universe, who hast not made me a woman' (after similar thanksgiving to God for not having made them slaves or heathen). So God gave to the humble and weak, to those who in the eyes of their contemporaries were the least suitable for such honour, the privilege of being the first to receive the news of the Lord's resurrection. To the women – not the apostles! Those who had been specially appointed by Jesus to be with Him in His ministry, and to be His witnesses, and who were to be the leaders of the Church, were passed over at this time of all times, and had to learn of the Resurrection from the women. Calvin is very right in his commentary on the first three Gospels at this point when he refers us to Paul's words: 'but God chose the foolish things of the world, that he might put to shame them that are wise; and God chose the weak things of the world, that he might put to shame the things that are strong; and the base things of the world, and the things that are despised, did God choose, yea and the things that are not, that he might bring to nought the things that are: that no flesh should glory before God' (1 Corinthians 1.27–29).

When the women reached the tomb, they found to their surprise that the great stone which served to close the entrance to it had been 'rolled back'. (Many rock-tombs of various patterns have been discovered in the neighbourhood of Jerusalem.) 'And entering into the tomb, they saw a young man sitting on the right side, arrayed in a white robe . . .' There is no doubt that Mark means by 'a young man' an angel. Karl Barth has recently challenged the widespread tendency to dismiss the angels as mere pious fancy, an old-world superstition, and we shall be wise to heed him. But we should take his advice and very carefully distinguish the angels of the Bible from the far from convincing 'angels' of most Christian art! Throughout the central part of the gospel story we hear practically nothing of angels. It is at the beginning and at the end that they appear. Their presence is an indication that we are concerned with an event, which, while it really happened, really took place in the course of history, was nevertheless not of the same texture as the rest of history, but was unique, and therefore not verifiable by ordinary historical methods. So, the Incarnation and the Resurrection, while they were certainly actual events that happened, and in that sense fully historical, were not simply of a piece with the rest of history. They are unique events. The presence of the angel (or, rather, the angel's being seen) had the effect of characterizing them as unique, as of a different texture from ordinary history, although actually taking place in the course of history. So here the presence of the angel served to make clear to the women both the infinite mystery and majesty, the distance from them, of the event which had just taken place, and also its infinite graciousness, its nearness to them. Human eyes were not permitted to witness the actual event of the Resurrection; but the angels as the constant witnesses of God's action did see it, and the angel at the tomb was, as it were, a mirror through which the women were allowed to see a reflection of that which human eyes might not see. He was the authentic and reliable link between the

Resurrection and the women; and he prepared the women for the sight of the risen Lord, so that, when they saw Him, they might not misunderstand. Verse 6 relates the angel's testimony to the Resurrection. 'And he saith unto them, Be not amazed: ye seek Jesus, the Nazarene, which hath been crucified: he is risen; he is not here: behold, the place where they laid him!' The words, 'he is risen; he is not here: behold the place where they laid him' bear witness to the fact that the tomb was empty. They attest the Resurrection as really *resurrection*: that is, they testify that the meaning of the Resurrection is, not that the Jesus whom the women had loved somehow lives on as an inspiration or even as an immortal spirit, but that He has been raised up by God in the fullness of His personal life, both body and soul. His grave is empty. His body was indeed transformed; for apparently He was able to pass through closed doors (compare John 20.19, 26) and to appear and disappear at will; but the New Testament emphasizes the truth that it was the same body as that which was crucified (e.g. John 20.27). The words of the angel attest nothing less than this.

But there was more that the angel said. As well as bearing witness to the fact of the Lord's resurrection, he gave the women a message to deliver to the disciples: 'But go, tell his disciples and Peter, He goeth before you into Galilee: there shall ye see him, as he said unto you.' The special mention of Peter was no doubt intended as an assurance of restoration to the disciple, who after his denial of Jesus was in special need of restoration and reassurance. The content of the message is apparently a promise of a resurrection appearance to the disciples in Galilee; and it is natural to assume that, had Mark finished his Gospel, he would have included an account of it. But, as the Revised Version margin and the Revised Standard Version and New English Bible make clear, verse 8 is the last verse of the Gospel as Mark wrote it; verses 9–20 are a summary not originally written to form the end of a gospel, but for a different purpose (probably as a summary to be used in the training of candidates for baptism) and then inserted here to fill the obvious gap. Mark was apparently in some way or other prevented from finishing his Gospel. (The view that Mark intended to end the Gospel at verse 8 is extremely improbable.)

Verse 8 is specially interesting. The statement, 'they said nothing to any one', is a very surprising sequel to the angel's command recorded in the previous verse. It is peculiar to Mark. Both Matthew and Luke give the sort of sequel we should expect: Matthew that the women 'ran to bring his disciples word', Luke that they 'returned from the tomb, and told all these things to the eleven, and to all the rest'. Presumably Mark meant his words to be understood in a limited sense – that their silence was only for a little while. But he gives special prominence to this silence of the women. So it is something which requires explanation.

Mark himself gives the reason in the words, 'for they were afraid'. It is quite unlikely that Mark is referring to fear of the Jews or fear of not being believed or of being thought mad, as some have suggested; for Mark has already piled up words expressing fear and amazement in these verses – 'they were amazed', 'be not amazed', 'fled', 'trembling', and 'astonishment'; and these clearly refer to the fear aroused by their experience at the tomb. We must therefore surely assume that the statement that 'they were afraid' refers to this same fear. It is also mentioned in Matthew: 'Fear not ye', says the angel to the women in 28.5, and in 28.8 we are told that the women departed from the tomb 'with fear and great joy', and in Luke 24.5 we read that 'they were affrighted'. But it is not so stressed either in Matthew or in Luke as it is in Mark. What then is the meaning of this 'fear'?

It was fear of *God*. The women had seen the traces of God's direct intervention. Through the mirror of the angel's witness they had seen the reflection of the eschatological[1] action of God. No wonder that they were afraid. Mark's emphasis on this fear is a very necessary antidote to all sentimentalizing of Easter. It points to the fact that the reassurance which the Easter message brings is a reassurance on the other side of a radical disturbing of all our security and self-assurance. The 'great joy' of which Matthew speaks lies on the far side of this 'fear' and 'amazement', and an Easter joy that is on this side of it is likely to be bogus. For here is something which calls in question the things which we are apt to take for granted. This is no mere resuscitation of a Lazarus, though that is disturbing enough! This is not a restoration to a life that once more must succumb to death. This is indeed the final resurrection brought forward in time, for Christ is 'the firstfruits of them that are asleep' (1 Corinthians 15.20). But in one way or another we try to come to terms with the resurrection of Jesus, to strike a bargain with it, so to speak, on what we fondly think are advantageous terms. We try to treat it as a familiar piece of our mental furniture, to make ourselves think that we are quite at home with it. We may perhaps regard it as a sort of emblem of man's immortality or connect it with the annual renewal of nature in the spring. Easter has suffered almost, if not quite, as much as Christmas from its

[1] i.e., belonging to the end of history and the in-breaking of God's New Order.

'atmosphere' and 'associations'. Again and again, though in many different ways, we make the futile attempt to reduce God and God's action to the measure of our mental capacity and emotional convenience. It may be by preaching about the beauties of spring – but spring is a particularly unfortunate illustration of Easter, for it illustrates something altogether different from that which the gospel proclaims; for spring is followed by summer and autumn and then winter, new life by a further dying, whereas 'Christ being raised from the dead dieth no more' (Romans 6.9), and the one thing is something general and natural and familiar, while the other is the miracle that turns the world upside down. Or it may be by drawing off attention on to the 'atmosphere' and associations, as when a church advertises its Easter services as a 'festival of white flowers'! Mark's account just does not fit into this sort of picture at all: for in the sentimentalized Easter there is no room for that fear to which he gives such prominence. If all that the women had seen was the token of a particular instance of some general principle, an illustration of life after death after the fashion of the spring, or anything of that sort, they would hardly have fled in such terror. What they had seen was the token, the traces, of the direct and altogether decisive intervention of God. So Mark's account (more emphatically than any of the others) warns us against trying to by-pass the fear or ignore it. The message of Easter is indeed a message of real, triumphant, present joy, but joy in the context of this fear and awe.

But what does it mean for us here and now? It means that God, the eternal and mysterious God, has really manifested Himself in Jesus of Nazareth. Of course we believe as Christians that He was truly revealing Himself in the whole of Christ's earthly life and in His death on the cross. But it is only from the standpoint, only in the light, of Easter that this becomes clear. The Resurrection stamps the whole life, ministry and death of Jesus Christ as revelation of the living God. For in raising Him from the dead, God intervened directly and decisively to vindicate His Son. Easter authenticates Jesus as no mere prophet or teacher or saint, but the self-manifestation of the eternal and holy God.

It means that we are justified. The Resurrection is God's seal upon the cross of Christ as man's redemption. It brings to light the true meaning of the Cross, the meaning which was hidden until the Crucified was raised on the third day. The message of Easter is not a new message over and above the message of Good Friday, but rather the revelation of the true meaning of Good Friday. The Resurrection reveals the death of Jesus as His victory over Satan and death and sin. It makes it clear that on the cross He was not only bearing the sin of the world, but bearing it away successfully, so that 'There is . . . now no condemnation to them that are in Christ Jesus' (Romans 8.1). The Son of God has borne our sin for us, and borne it away.

It means that we may live. It is the guarantee that God's purpose for us is that we should share Christ's risen life. It is the pledge of our resurrection, the assurance that, when we die, our souls shall be with Christ, and at the last day God shall raise our bodies to glory, so that our personal life, transformed and renewed but in its true completeness, shall share for ever the glory of Jesus Christ.

It means that our present life in its fullness is claimed by God for Himself, that we are claimed for gratitude, for obedience. The fact that He who is our Lord to whom we belong both body and soul has been raised up by the power of the Father means inescapably that we are obliged to 'walk in newness of life' (Romans 6.4), to reckon ourselves 'dead unto sin, but alive unto God in Christ Jesus' (Romans 6.11).

What we have to do now is to pray God to give us true faith, so that to the Easter message 'Christ is risen!' we may truly and believingly, in heart and life, respond, 'He is risen indeed!'

> Almighty God, who through thine only-begotten Son Jesus Christ hast overcome death, and opened unto us the gate of everlasting life: We humbly beseech thee, that as by thy special grace preventing us thou dost put into our minds good desires, so by thy continual help we may bring the same to good effect; through Jesus Christ our Lord, who liveth and reigneth with thee and the Holy Ghost, ever one God, world without end. Amen.
>
> (Collect for Easter Day)

7

ASCENSION

... Jesus Christ; who is on the right hand of God, having gone into heaven ...

(1 Peter 3.21–22)

The text speaks of two actions: the one it represents as having taken place in the past, the other as continuing in the present.

I

We shall consider first *that part of the text which refers to the past*. The apostle speaks of Jesus Christ as 'having gone into heaven'. The New Testament has various ways of referring to this event. It speaks, for example, of Christ's going to His Father (e.g. John 14.12 and 28), of His ascending (e.g. John 3.13; 20.17: cf. Acts 2.34), of His exaltation (e.g. Acts 2.33; Philippians 2.9), of His being received up (e.g. Acts 1.2, 11; 1 Timothy 3.16). It is not necessary to assume that this going into heaven is simply to be identified with what is related in Acts 1.9–11. We should probably rather think of what is related there as the outward sign and wonder which pointed to, testified to, the event, unseen by mortal eyes, of the return of the Son of God to the glory of His Father, but which was not itself that event (just as the event of the Virgin Birth was the outward sign and wonder which pointed to, and bore witness to, the event of the Incarnation, but was not identical with that event). Acts 1.9–11 relates the ending of the last of the resurrection appearances of Jesus. The other appearances had ended in the vanishing of Jesus. But there was about the ending of this last appearance that which was distinctive, which gave the apostles to understand both that this appearance was final, that they were not to expect more such appearances till the Final Coming, and also that the Lord's departure was a departure to heaven, a return to the glory of the Father.

The actual event of the Ascension, to which the ending of the last of the Resurrection appearances pointed, has a twofold meaning. On the one hand, it has what might be called a negative significance. It is the Lord's going away from His disciples, the fulfilment of His words recorded in Mark 14.7, 'For ye have the poor always with you . . .: but me ye have not always.' It marks the beginning of that time throughout which, while He truly keeps His promise, 'Lo, I am with you always, even unto the end of the world' (Matthew 28.20), coming again and again to His disciples indirectly and hiddenly, through the Holy Spirit, in Word and Sacrament and in the suffering humanity of His needy brethren, He is also in a real sense absent from them (compare the parable of the Absent Master in Mark 13.34–36). It marks the beginning of the time, during which He is no longer with His disciples in the way in which He was with them in the days of His earthly ministry, and not yet with them as He will be in the final reunion, the beginning of the time in which the Church has to 'walk by faith, not by sight' (2 Corinthians 5.7). It marks the end of the period of revelation, and warns against all foolish dreams of a further divine self-revelation which goes beyond the one Word of God which is Jesus Christ our Lord. The promise in John 16.13 that the Holy Spirit 'shall guide you into all the truth' means, as the context makes clear, not that He is going to reveal some further truth which is independent of Jesus Christ, but that He will lead the disciples into an ever fuller understanding of Him who in His own person is 'the truth' (John 14.6).

And, on the other hand, the Ascension, this going into heaven, of which the text speaks, has a positive significance. It is the transition from the conditions and limitations of life in this world to the freedom and unrestricted effectiveness of Christ's exalted life, His translation from this world to the world of glory. It is clearly this positive significance which the apostle has here chiefly in mind; for his main interest in this verse is in the continuing exalted life of Christ, and he only refers to His going into heaven in a dependent participial clause. When its positive significance is understood, the Ascension, though it means Christ's going away from us, is reason for joy. That is why the apostles, according to Luke 24.52, after Jesus' parting from them, 'returned to Jerusalem with great joy', and not overwhelmed with forlornness, as one might have expected.

II

We turn now to *the part of the text which refers to the present.* Peter speaks of Jesus Christ 'who is at the right hand of God . . .' Paul in Romans 8.34 uses the same language. Elsewhere the New Testament tends to speak of His *sitting* at the right hand of God. Thus Mark 16.19 states magnificently, 'So then the Lord Jesus, after he had spoken unto them, was received up into heaven, and sat down at the right hand of God'; the Epistle to the Hebrews speaks of Christ as having 'sat down on the right hand of the Majesty on high' (Hebrews 1.3: cf. 8.1; 10.12;

12.2); and Paul exhorts the Colossians to 'seek the things that are above, where Christ is, seated on the right hand of God' (Colossians 3.1). The Creeds take up the language of the New Testament. At this point the Apostles' Creed has the words, 'And sitteth on the right hand of God the Father Almighty', and the Nicene Creed, 'And sitteth on the right hand of the Father'. Behind the use of this language which speaks of Jesus as being or sitting on the right hand of God is the influence of Psalm 110.1, 'The LORD saith unto my Lord, Sit thou at my right hand, Until I make thine enemies thy footstool.'

That this is picture-language, derived from the customary practice of oriental courts in which the king's chief minister would sit or stand at the king's right hand, need hardly be said. It was clearly seen by Calvin, for instance, who, with reference to this clause in the Apostles' Creed, says: 'The comparison is drawn from kings who have assessors at their side to whom they delegate the tasks of ruling and governing' and, again, 'it is a question, not of the disposition of his body, but of the majesty of his authority'.[1] To be or sit on the right hand of God is to be invested with the full majesty and authority of God.

The fact that Psalm 110.1 seems to be quoted or echoed in the New Testament more frequently than any other Old Testament verse is an indication that the focal point of the early Church's faith was this 'heavenly session' of Christ; and the fact that the earliest creed of the Church was *Kurios Iesous*, that is, 'Jesus is Lord' (cf. Romans 10.9; 1 Corinthians 12.3; 2 Corinthians 4.5; Philippians 2.11) points in the same direction. St Paul, indeed, tells the

---

[1] *Institutes of the Christian Religion*, II. xvi.15 (quoted according to the translation of F. L. Battles (London, 1961).

Corinthians that he had 'determined not to know anything among' them, 'save Jesus Christ, and him crucified' (1 Corinthians 2.2); but when Paul preached Christ crucified, he preached, not a Christ who was still on the cross, a dying, or a dead, Christ, but the exalted crucified One, the Christ who had died on the cross but was now alive and glorified and Lord of all.

There is one other thing which must be said before we pass on to a consideration of what this heavenly session of Christ means for us. It concerns the question, What is it that is new in Christ's sitting on the right hand of God? It is, of course, true that the eternal Son of God was possessed from all eternity of the authority and glory of His Father. And in His earthly life He was still possessed of them – as the eternal Son of God. So Calvin, commenting on Matthew 17.9, says: '. . . even during the time that he emptied himself (Philippians 2.7), he continued to retain his divinity entire, though it was concealed under the veil of the flesh.' And the same point is expressed in a rather more difficult way in the hymn of St Thomas Aquinas:

'The Word of God, proceeding forth
Yet leaving not his Father's side, . . .'[1]

But both in His pre-existence and in the days of His earthly life it was as the eternal Son of God that He was possessed of the divine glory and power. The new thing in His heavenly session is that now He is invested with God's majesty and authority and glory not only as the eternal Son of God, but also as Man, as our Brother. For He is still Man as well as God. His manhood was not a

[1] *The English Hymnal*, hymn 330.

temporary dwelling adopted for a while, then to be laid aside; it was assumed for ever.

What then does this heavenly session of Jesus Christ mean for us?

First, He is *our Forerunner*. In Hebrews 6.20 the word 'forerunner' is actually used: '. . . within the veil; whither as a forerunner Jesus entered for us . . .' And in John 14.2 Jesus says to His disciples: 'I go to prepare a place for you.' His present glory is the pledge of our glory to be, the assurance that, if we now suffer with Him, we shall hereafter share His glory (Romans 8.17). So the Heidelberg Catechism (Question 49) includes among the benefits which we have from Christ's ascension: 'that we have our flesh in Heaven, as a sure pledge that He, as the Head, will also take us, His members, up to Himself.'[1]

Secondly, He is *our High Priest* – a truth specially prominent in the Epistle to the Hebrews. It is through Him that we approach God. That sinners should have access to the holy God is no matter of course. To treat it as such would be to insult God's majesty and goodness. But in Christ our High Priest we have forgiveness – through His availing sacrifice, His atonement. As the Jewish High Priest entered into the Holy of Holies, so Christ has entered into the very presence of God in heaven. But, whereas the Jewish High Priest sprinkled the blood of an animal victim on the mercy-seat, Christ has entered by virtue of His own precious blood shed for the sins of all mankind, 'through his own blood', as Hebrews 9.12 puts it. And, unlike the Jewish High Priest, He had no need to offer 'as for the people, so also for himself' (Hebrews 5.3), since He was sinless. Again, unlike the Jewish High Priest, who entered once a year, Christ has gone in 'once for all'

[1] T. F. Torrance, *The School of Faith*, London, 1959, p. 77.

(Hebrews 9.12; cf. 9.25f, 28). His one sacrifice has never to be repeated; for He has offered – in the words of the Book of Common Prayer – 'a full, perfect and sufficient sacrifice, oblation and satisfaction, for the sins of the whole world'.

And having made atonement for us, He abides for ever 'before the face of God for us' (Hebrews 9.24). 'And if any man sin', says 1 John 2.1f, 'we have an Advocate with the Father, Jesus Christ the righteous: and he is the propitiation for our sins; and not for ours only, but also for the whole world.' This is His work of intercession, of which Paul speaks: 'It is Christ Jesus that died, yea rather, that was raised from the dead, who is at the right hand of God, who also maketh intercession for us' (Romans 8.34). Says the writer to the Hebrews: 'Wherefore also he is able to save to the uttermost them that draw near unto God through him, seeing he ever liveth to make intercession for them' (Hebrews 7.25). I remember sometimes during the short period that I was in action in the Second World War being too pressed and too weary to pray with proper concentration and hoping that someone at home might be praying for me. The heavenly session of Christ means that a more effective prayer even than that of a loved one at home is being offered for each one of us continually. And it is being offered by One who understands our temptations and sorrows from the inside, so to speak. 'For we have not a high priest', says the writer to the Hebrews, 'that cannot be touched with the feeling of our infirmities; but one that hath been in all points tempted like as we are, yet without sin' (Hebrews 4.15).

The full significance of Christ's high priesthood is perhaps most clearly hinted at in Colossians 3.1 and 3: 'If then ye were raised together with Christ, seek the things that are above, where Christ is, seated on the right hand of God . . . For ye died, and your life is hid with Christ in God.' The exalted Christ does not only pray for us; He lives for us. There is here a fundamental divine decision to see us in Christ, so that the life which we are now living in its frailty and sinfulness is in God's sight dead and done with, a thing of the past, and the life which Jesus Christ is living for us at God's right hand is our real life, the life which God in His mercy has decided to recognize as our life. This is what William Bright's hymn means, when it says:

'Look, Father, look on His anointed face,
And only look on us as found in Him'.[1]

It is in this sense – and, of course, only in this sense – that we may rightly speak of a sinless perfection of Christians!

Thirdly, He is *King*. All authority in heaven and on earth has already been given to Him (Matthew 28.18). God has put all things under His feet (Hebrews 2.8). But that same passage of Hebrews goes on to say: 'But now we see not yet all things subjected to him.' His kingship is not yet acknowledged by all. It is still in this world a hidden, veiled kingship, which can only be recognized by faith. But it is none the less real. His heavenly session means that, in spite of all that here on earth seems to deny His kingship, He is already King of all, and His enemies have no chance of final victory, though in the meantime they may do much damage.

He is King of the Church. God 'has appointed Him universal and supreme Head of the Church' (Ephesians 1.22 in Weymouth's translation). Ascension Day has not

[1] *The Church Hymnary* (3rd ed.), hymn 580.

counted for much in recent years in our English Free
Churches. It is not a Sunday and not a Bank Holiday. So
we are apt to ignore it. In most of our congregations there
is no service on Ascension Day. We may, or we may not,
remember the ascension and heavenly session of Christ on
the following Sunday. Yet of all Christians in England we
ought most to be stirred by its message: for it was for the
crown rights of the Redeemer in His Church that our
fathers witnessed and suffered, protesting against their
infringement whether by bishops or by the civil
government. He is a King who expects to be obeyed, who
expects His subjects to take His kingship seriously, not
just to proclaim it piously, but to act upon it (Luke
6.46–49). In the Church the questions, 'What does the
minister wish?', 'What does the session wish?', 'What do
the members of the congregation wish?', are all equally
irrelevant and improper. The question to be asked is
rather 'What do you judge to be the will of Jesus Christ
the King and Head of the Church?' It is that question
which minister and session and the members of the
congregation are alike challenged to answer in full
personal responsibility to the exalted Christ.

And it is by His Word that He wills to govern His
Church – by Scripture, which is His royal sceptre. As the
sheep know their shepherd's voice and follow him, and
will not follow strangers (John 10.4f), so it is the mark of
those who belong to Christ that they recognize their
King's voice and obey Him. Whether what we do meets
with success or failure – that is not our responsibility but
Christ's. Our responsibility is simply to obey Him. But
that will involve being ready to be disturbed and driven
out of old, comfortable, and reassuringly familiar ruts,
and to go out into strange places at His command, as
Abraham 'went out, not knowing whither he went'

(Hebrews 11.8); it will involve allowing Him freely to judge and criticize us, forgive and heal, guide and strengthen, and not trying to keep Him within the framework of an agenda chosen by us.

He is also King of the world. The Church is but the inner circle of His dominion, the area in which His kingship is known and acknowledged. Beyond its frontiers His authority, though it is not yet known and acknowledged, is no less real – His writ runs and His laws apply. He is already 'the ruler of the kings of the earth' (Revelation 1.5), the 'Lord of lords, and King of kings' (Revelation 17.14; 19.16), to whom 'all authority hath been given . . . in heaven and on earth' (Matthew 28.18); and consciously or unconsciously, willingly or unwillingly, directly or indirectly, the governments of the nations subserve His royal will. The whole of the world's life is the object of His concern, His judgment and His mercy. When the Christian passes into the world beyond the frontiers of the Church, he is not stepping out of His Lord's realm into the realm of some other lord: he is still within the dominion of Jesus Christ. To remember this is to know that when the Church has to confront governments and nations in defence of justice and truth and humanity, it is a matter of calling to order in the name of the King of kings those who are already His subjects, albeit rebellious. When from time to time 'Church leaders' remember this, they lose their proneness to wait cap in hand at the back-doors of governments, and are enabled to speak out clearly and unambiguously in the name of Jesus Christ.

Almighty God, who hast exalted Thy Son Jesus Christ to Thy right hand, we give Thee thanks that He has entered into Thy glory to prepare a place for us, that He ever lives to intercede for us, and that Thou hast made Him to be the only King and Head of Thy Church, and the Ruler of the kings of the earth. Grant that we may not only proclaim His kingship with our lips but may also acknowledge it in our lives, so that at the last we may come to that place which He has prepared for us. We ask it in His Name, who is our High Priest, Jesus Christ our Lord. Amen.

8

PENTECOST

... but tarry ye in the city, until ye be clothed with power from on high.

(Luke 24.49b.)

... but ye received the Spirit[1] of adoption, whereby we cry, Abba, Father.

(Romans 8.15b.)

These are two texts which throw light upon each other. The former speaks about 'power'. It is a word which we often use. We talk about power politics, naval power, air power, about the Great Powers; on a different plane we talk about horse-power, electric power and now nuclear power. We all think we know quite a lot about power. We also know – even though we may not like to talk about it – a lot about lack of power, about our own powerlessness. For example, when the follies of the statesmen of the world look as though they are leading us inevitably to the abyss, which of us is not painfully conscious of the slightness of our power as individuals to do anything to prevent the nations rushing headlong into catastrophe? But it is quite clear that the text is speaking about a different power, a power that is not under the control of men, not something that scientists can master and statesmen exploit. It is – so the text makes clear – something that comes 'from on high'. It is the risen Jesus

[1] The Revised Version has 'spirit', but 'Spirit' (as in the New English Bible) is surely to be preferred.

who is speaking to His disciples, and He is saying that He is going to send forth upon them the Holy Spirit which the Father has promised. The power is the power of the Holy Spirit. What strange sort of power is this?

Let us turn first to the Romans passage to see what light it has to give. Paul is also speaking about the Holy Spirit. Though he does not use the word 'power', he does indicate very precisely what this power is! He indicates it more clearly, I think, than St Luke does in his Pentecost narrative – at least he indicates it in a way which we can probably more easily understand. Here he calls the Holy Spirit 'the Spirit of adoption, whereby we cry, Abba, Father'. And he goes on to say that 'the Spirit himself beareth witness with our spirit, that we are children of God'. So Paul defines this power, of which Jesus had spoken, as the power to call God 'Father'. And ultimately you and I do not know much about power until we know *this* power. It is something quite different from all that the world means by power. What, then, is this power to call God 'Father'?

It is first of all power to believe in Jesus Christ, to recognize in Jesus of Nazareth the Son of the living God, our Saviour and Lord, and to trust ourselves to Him; for there is no really significant calling God 'Father' apart from, except through, faith in Jesus Christ. Plenty of men, of course, have talked, and no doubt plenty do still talk, about God as Father without reference to Jesus Christ. The heathen have often called their chief god 'Father'. In the *Iliad* and *Odyssey* of Homer, the expression 'Father both of men and of gods' is a stereotyped phrase, coming again and again. But this calling God 'Father' apart from Christ is merely human wishful thinking. Of course, in our consciousness of our weakness and defencelessness, we men would naturally like to feel that there is Someone great and strong – almighty in fact – who is kindly disposed to us. This is a very natural human desire, to want a great big father to take care of one and defend one against dangers known and unknown. But the question is whether I really have the right to call the true, the living, holy God, 'Father'. It is only through Jesus Christ that we can know the true God – 'No one cometh unto the Father, but by me', said Jesus (John 14.6); and only through Him that we who are impure sinners can have the right to call this holy God 'Father'. So the answer to the 26th question of the Heidelberg Catechism runs: 'That the eternal Father of our Lord Jesus Christ ... is for the sake of Christ His Son my God and Father ...' This power to call God 'Father' which the Holy Spirit gives is, then, in contrast to all mere human wishful thinking about an omnipotent father, the right, through Jesus Christ, to call the one true, holy and living God 'our Father'. We have no right to tell ourselves that we are God's children. This is something which we have to be told. And it is only significant when told to us on the highest authority, that is, by God Himself.

And, secondly, it is power to know God through Christ as our loving Father, and so to be able to commit ourselves to Him wholly with utter confidence. It is freedom to trust God, to know that our lives are safe in His hands, and that 'to them that love God all things work together for good'(Romans 8.28).

But, in the third place, to call this holy God 'Father' really meaningfully and sincerely involves desiring wholeheartedly to be and think and speak and do what is well-pleasing to Him, what fits in with calling Him 'Father', and to avoid doing whatever is displeasing to Him, whatever is inconsistent with calling Him 'Father'. And the power to which the text from Luke refers is power thus meaningfully to call God 'Father'. We may put this in another way by saying, as Paul is doing in Romans 8, that the Holy Spirit is the One who re-establishes God's law in its true character for us, freeing it from its abuse and perversion by human legalism, from men's attempts to twist it into something complimentary to their own pride and self-righteousness and complacency, and re-establishing it as God's holy law – not merely the law of God the supreme King and Lord, but also, and above all, as the law of God our loving Father, the revelation of His fatherly will for His children, and, therefore, something which we can accept gladly as a gracious gift from His fatherly hands. It is true that even Christians who have God's Holy Spirit fall very far short of fulfilling the requirements of this gracious law, this fatherly will of God for His children. But they do ever more and more wholeheartedly desire to fulfil it and to walk in the way of His commandments; they are turned in the direction of obedience, even though their clinging sins make them sometimes drag their feet and go but slowly, instead of running (Psalm 119.32), in the way of God's commandments. This being turned in the direction of obedience, having a sincere desire to obey, is the hallmark of a Christian. Paul says in Romans 8.9: 'If any man hath not the Spirit of Christ, he is none of his.' 'Those in whom the Spirit does not reign', says Calvin, 'do not belong to Christ . . . We must always bear in mind the counsel of the apostle, that free remission of sins cannot be separated from the Spirit of regeneration. This would be, as it were, to rend Christ asunder.' Christ cannot be sundered from His own Spirit, and the man who does not manifest the presence of the Holy Spirit by this being turned in the direction of obedience to God's law, cannot rightly be called a Christian.

An important part of this obedience has to do with God's other children. To avoid what is displeasing to God certainly involves avoiding all that is detrimental to His other children, and to seek after what is pleasing to Him and consistent with calling Him 'Father' involves seeking the good of His other children. The very plurals which Paul uses here ('ye received' and 'we cry') imply that God is the Father of a family, and that in calling Him 'Father' we dare not forget the rest of the family. And this is of course brought home to us by the prayer the Lord Himself gave us: '*Our* Father . . . Give *us* this day *our* daily bread; and forgive *us* . . .' To quote Calvin once more – 'Let the Christian, then, so regulate his prayers as to make them common, and embrace all who are his brethren in Christ; not only those whom at present he sees and knows to be such, but all men who are alive upon the earth.'[1] To call God 'Father' seriously (in the sense which St Paul means) involves caring for our fellow men. For example, those in this country who truly call God 'Father' by the power of the Holy Spirit will be concerned for the two thirds of the world's population who are either starving or seriously under-nourished; they will not be able callously to enjoy the prosperity of the nation that has 'never had it so good' without caring for those in other lands who are hungry.

In the fourth place, seriously to call God 'Father' involves bearing witness to Jesus Christ before others; for God is not content to be the Father only of those who now are Christians; He desires to be the Father of all men. To call Him 'Father' therefore, entails being concerned that the children of God who are scattered abroad may be gathered into one. So in the context of our text from Luke

[1] *Institutes of the Christian Religion*, III, xx.38 (quoted according to the translation of H. Beveridge, London, 1949).

– in verse 48 Jesus says: 'Ye are *witnesses* of these things.' And in Acts 1.8 the receiving of power is explicitly associated with bearing witness – 'ye shall receive power, when the Holy Ghost is come upon you: and ye shall be my witnesses. . . .' Those who cry 'Abba, Father' sincerely and by the power of the Holy Spirit know that they are under an obligation to bear witness to Jesus Christ as the Lord and Saviour of all mankind.

In view of what we have so far seen, do we not all of us have to ask ourselves quite seriously: 'Do I really call God "Father" – in this serious, significant sense?' We shall all of us have to confess that there are, at any rate, serious deficiencies and inconsistencies in our calling Him 'Father', and that only very haltingly and stammeringly do we so address Him.

Now that we have seen from the Romans passage something of what this power, of which our Lord spoke, means, we are in a position to realize more truly and accurately our own powerlessness, the weakness of our faith in Jesus Christ, our doubts about God's fatherly care and hesitations about trusting ourselves to Him, our lack of a whole-hearted desire to please Him and to live lives that are consistent with calling Him 'Father', our failure sincerely and gladly to recognize His other children, the feebleness and inadequacy of our witness before the world. Must we not confess that our lives have a good deal in common with the dry bones of Ezekiel's vision (Ezekiel 37); that the boldness which the apostles displayed after the day of Pentecost (Acts 4.13, 29, 31; 28.31) and the confidence which distinguished the early Church are sadly lacking in us; that we are somehow tongue-tied and timid, lacking in decisiveness, and unable to communicate the gospel effectively?

At this point it is well to turn back to the Luke passage.

For in its turn it has light to throw upon the Pauline text. It speaks of waiting – 'tarry ye in the city, until ye be clothed with power from on high'. This power was something for which the disciples had to wait. The gap between the ascension of our Lord and the Day of Pentecost has theological and practical significance for us. It underlines the truth that even our response to God's mighty deed for our redemption, our response to the grace of God in Christ, is not something that we accomplish by our own strength. Luther in his catechism says: 'I believe that I cannot by my own reason or strength believe in Jesus Christ my Lord or come to Him.' And this is true. The power of which our Luke text speaks, the power which, we have learnt from Paul, is the power to call God 'Father', to call the true and living God through Jesus Christ His only Son 'our Father', is something which we cannot grasp for ourselves – it has to be given to us 'from on high', and to emphasize that it has to be given, we have to wait.

What then does it mean for us to 'tarry in the city', to wait for God's gift of power from on high?

We must acknowledge our weakness and ineffectiveness and give up trying to keep up our own spirits by pretending we are stronger than we are. We must acknowledge our emptiness, and then in true penitence acknowledge that that emptiness is something for which we are to blame, because so often we have spurned God's power, preferring to use our own, and have thought we were going to manage nicely with our own resources; and because we have so often grieved God's Holy Spirit and driven Him from our hearts. And then in humility and expectation we must ask for God's forgiveness and for the gift of His Holy Spirit. God will not fail to hear the prayers of those who sincerely ask Him

to give them His Holy Spirit. Jesus said: 'If ye then, being
evil, know how to give good gifts unto your children, how
much more shall your heavenly Father give the Holy
Spirit to them that ask him?' (Luke 11.13).

Come, holy Spirit, heav'nly Dove,
    With all Thy quick'ning pow'rs,
Kindle a flame of sacred love
    In these cold hearts of ours.

In vain we tune our formal songs,
    In vain we strive to rise,
Hosannas languish on our tongues
    And our devotion dies.

Dear Lord! and shall we ever live
    At this poor dying rate,
Our love so faint, so cold to Thee,
    And thine to us so great?

Come, holy Spirit, heav'nly Dove,
    With all Thy quick'ning pow'rs,
Come, shed abroad a Saviour's love,
    And that shall kindle ours. Amen.

(Isaac Watts, *Hymns and Spiritual Songs in Three Books*,
London, 1788, Book II, hymn xxxiv, verses 1, 3, 4 and 5.)

9

EPILOGUE

If God *is* for us, who *is* against us? (Romans 8.31).

These words might be said to sum up all the other words of Scripture to which we have been trying to listen; and their exposition may well serve as an epilogue to this short series.

What a splendid confidence they express! It is the confidence which resounds magnificently through the whole of the last paragraph of Romans 8, and reaches a climax in Paul's declaration: 'For I am persuaded, that neither death, nor life, nor angels, nor principalities, nor things present, nor things to come, nor powers, nor height, nor depth, nor any other creature, shall be able to separate us from the love of God, which is in Christ Jesus our Lord.' But do not many of us feel a certain wistfulness as we listen to such sentences of the apostle, a sense that this is the sort of confidence and certainty to be expected in apostles and such great Christians of the past as the Reformers, but which is somehow not for us? The question which we have to ask ourselves in the face of this text and in the light of the other passages we have been considering is: Does anything less than this confidence of the apostle Paul measure up to the gospel? Does not the gospel itself demand just such a confidence and certainty?

The 'if' at the beginning of this text is not an ordinary 'if' introducing a conditional clause stating a condition which may or may not be fulfilled. It reflects a Greek idiom according to which 'if' can be used to state a fact as the ground of an argument or appeal, where English would normally use 'since' or 'seeing that'. So there is nothing hypothetical about the clause 'if God is for us'. Paul does not mean 'supposing that God is for us', but 'since God is for us'. He is stating what he is altogether convinced is a fact as the ground of the confidence expressed in the rhetorical question, 'who is against us?'

St Paul is speaking about *God*. When he says, 'If God is for us, . . .', he is not referring to a god of man's imagination, of man's wishful thinking, a god made in man's image and for man's convenience, but of the one, true, living God, to whom the Scriptures bear witness, the God of revelation, the God who has revealed Himself in Jesus Christ His only Son, and by His Holy Spirit has enabled men to receive His self-revelation and to respond to it.

When Paul uses the word 'God' here, he is no doubt thinking particularly of God the Father. But in this eighth chapter of Romans he has spoken of God 'sending his own Son' (verse 3), and not sparing His own Son (verse 32); he has also spoken of 'the Spirit of life' (verse 2), who is also 'the Spirit of God' (verses 9 and 14) and 'the Spirit of Christ' (verse 9), who dwells in Christians, helps their infirmity, and makes intercession for them according to God's will. At this point, therefore, while it is true that Paul nowhere sets forth a doctrine of the Trinity, we cannot avoid the Church's doctrine of the Trinity, if we are to bring out the meaning of his words faithfully. We are compelled to say that this God, who according to the Bible has revealed Himself through, and in, His only-begotten Son, and by His Holy Spirit has made men participators in His self-revelation, is Father, Son and Holy Spirit, not merely in His act of self-revelation, but in Himself – eternally. The Son is only able to reveal the Father because He is Himself eternal God, inseparable from the Father, though distinguishable from Him; and the Spirit can only bring about our participation in God's self-revelation because He is Himself, equally with the Father and the Son, eternal God, inseparable from the Father and the Son, though distinguishable from them. When the Church confesses its faith in God, the Father, Son and Holy Spirit, One God in Three Persons (or three eternal modes of existence), the Triune God, the blessed and holy Trinity, it is acknowledging and confessing Him as the One He has shown Himself to be. Here we have to do not with a cleverly spun web of human speculation (human reason left to itself would surely have formulated a less baffling doctrine), but with a humble following of God's self-revelation.

It is this God, the God who in love created all things visible and invisible, but not because He lacked an object for His love (for in Himself, in His own triune existence and quite independently of our being there to be loved, He is from all eternity love, and behind His love for us men is the eternal love between the Father and the Son and the Holy Spirit), who 'is for us' – on our side.

But how do we know that He is for us? What is the ground of Paul's certainty that God is for us? Not the world around us, not nature – despite the assertions of some hymn-writers! For, while sunsets and sky-larks, calm seas and daffodils, may point to the existence of a benevolent Creator, there are other things in nature such as cobras and cancer, earthquakes and hurricanes, droughts and floods, which cannot be ignored. And the immensities of which modern science has made us aware are hardly in themselves reassuring. Paul himself was well aware of the existence of much in the world that is distressing. In this chapter he has spoken of the whole creation's having been subjected to vanity, and of its groaning and travailing in pain. The ground of his certainty that God is on our side was Jesus Christ, who had lived as a man among men, had suffered, had been crucified, dead and buried, who had 'been raised on the third day according to the scriptures', who had been exalted to God's right hand, and who now as Lord was ever active on behalf of His Church and of all mankind. And for us too Jesus Christ is the only, and the altogether sufficient, ground of confidence. On Trinity Sunday, when the Church looks back over the Christian Year from Advent to Pentecost and, as it adores the Triune God, seeks in so far as it is possible to hold together in its thought all the events of the gospel and to catch a glimpse of the wholeness of God's saving act, it has, as it were spread out before it, the evidence that 'God is for us'.

But to say that God is for us is not to say that we can use Him for our ends. He cannot be mobilized for the accomplishment of our purposes. He is for us, not as a subservient ally, but in His freedom and lordship. He is for us – as our Lord. He seeks that which in His wisdom He knows to be our true good, which is not always the same thing as that which we are convinced is good for us.

The last words of the text ('who is against us?') are a rhetorical question equivalent to an emphatic statement that there is no one whose hostility we need fear. Foes we indeed have, who are against us and seek our ruin; but with God on our side, we need not fear them. They may cause us to suffer, but they cannot snatch us out of His hand. There is nothing that can separate us from His love in Christ Jesus our Lord. This triumphant question was not asked by someone inexperienced in troubles. Consider the list of his sufferings in the eleventh chapter of 2 Corinthians. And in this last paragraph of Romans 8 he speaks of tribulation and anguish as one who knows them. But he knows that God is on our side, and that therefore we have no need to fear. All things that can happen to us He is able to turn to our good.

As we look back over the passages we have considered and over the saving events of the gospel to which they bear witness, and recognize that they tell us plainly that God the Father, Son and Holy Spirit, God in all the majesty and mystery of His being, is for us, on our side, can we do other than worship the majesty and mercy of this God and thank Him from the depths of our hearts for His goodness? Can we do other than give way to great joy and go on our way in confidence and hope, resolved to try to obey Him and live to His glory?

Most merciful God, who didst not spare Thine own Son, but deliveredst Him up for us all, grant that by the witness of Thy Holy Spirit we may surely know that Thou art for us; so that, facing the future without fear, we may gratefully and joyfully serve Thee, and be more than conquerors through Him that loved us, even Jesus Christ Thine only Son, our Lord and Saviour, who liveth and reigneth with Thee and the Holy Spirit, one God, for ever and ever. Amen.

PART II

The Good Samaritan and Other Sermons

·

1

THE GOOD SAMARITAN

And behold, a certain lawyer stood up and tempted him, saying, Master, what shall I do to inherit eternal life? And he said unto him, What is written in the law? how readest thou? And he answering said, Thou shalt love the Lord thy God with all thy heart, and with all thy soul, and with all thy strength, and with all thy mind; and thy neighbour as thyself. And he said unto him, Thou hast answered right: this do, and thou shalt live. But he, desiring to justify himself, said unto Jesus, And who is my neighbour? Jesus made answer and said, A certain man was going down from Jerusalem to Jericho; and he fell among robbers, which both stripped him and beat him, and departed, leaving him half dead. And by chance a certain priest was going down that way: and when he saw him, he passed by on the other side. And in like manner a Levite also, when he came to the place, and saw him, passed by on the other side. But a certain Samaritan, as he journeyed, came where he was; and when he saw him, he was moved with compassion, and came to him, and bound up his wounds, pouring on *them* oil and wine; and he set him on his own beast, and brought him to an inn, and took care of him. And on the morrow he took out two pence, and gave them to the host, and said, Take care of him; and whatsoever thou spendest more, I, when I come back again, will repay thee. Which of these three, thinkest thou, proved neighbour unto him that fell among the robbers?

> And he said, He that shewed mercy on him. And
> Jesus said unto him, Go, and do thou likewise.
>
> (Luke 10.25–37.)

The lawyer's question (Luke 10.25) is the same as that of the rich young ruler (Mark 10.17; Matthew 19.16; Luke 18.18), and Jesus in reply refers him to the law just as He does the ruler. The lawyer then sets together Deuteronomy 6.5 and Leviticus 19.18 as a summary of the law. It seems probable that the occasion referred to in Mark 12 and Matthew 22 was not the only one on which Jesus Himself did this, and it is possible that the lawyer in quoting the two texts was consciously expressing his agreement with something he knew Jesus was in the habit of saying, though perhaps with the intention of following this up with a request for more precise definition. At any rate, when Jesus says to him, 'Thou hast answered right: this do, and thou shalt live', he professes to want further guidance on the meaning of 'neighbour'. This is not surprising; for, while it was generally agreed that one's fellow-Israelites (including full-proselytes) were covered by the term, there was dispute as to where exactly the limits were to be drawn. By many the personal enemy was understood to be excluded (cf. Matthew 5.43), and the Pharisees tended to exclude all those Jews who did not live according to Pharisaic principles, the so-called 'people of the land'.

Jesus in reply tells the story of the man who fell among robbers on the road from Jerusalem to Jericho. He gives no definition of the term 'neighbour'; but His choice of a Samaritan to be the hero of His tale is an eloquent, though indirect, answer to the lawyer's question. He actually constrains the lawyer himself to admit that the Samaritan 'proved neighbour unto him that fell among the robbers' (verses 36–37) – though the lawyer avoids using the hated name 'Samaritan'! The implication is that there is no man whom we are not commanded to love; for, if the Samaritan, the outsider and enemy *par excellence*, can be a neighbour, then no one can be excluded. For the Jews' attitude to the Samaritans we may refer to 2 Kings 17.24ff; Ezra 4; Ecclesiasticus 50.25–26; John 4.9; 8.48. The relations between them had become very much more embittered in the time of Jesus as a result of an outrage by the Samaritans. One midnight during a Passover between A.D. 6 and A.D. 9 they had defiled the Temple court by scattering upon it dead men's bones. 'Samaritan' had, in fact, for the Jews of the time of Jesus something of the sort of flavour that 'Communist' has for the respectable citizens of Western Europe or the United States today. So 'neighbour', Jesus implies, must include even the outsider, the heretic, the enemy. A man is not to be excluded from this category because his religious confession or political creed or social background or the colour of his skin is different from our own.

By contrasting the Samaritan with a priest and a Levite Jesus further, incidentally, draws attention to a fact which the lawyer would doubtless prefer to forget – the fact that sometimes the outsider and the heretic and the heathen actually show mercy and lovingkindness, while those who claim to be the exponents of the true religion prove to be hard-hearted and loveless. The agnostic and the atheist sometimes behave better than the clergyman and the church-worker. It does not make sense, it ought not to be, but it happens; and it is good for us to be made to face facts, lest we build theories that do not fit the facts.

But the real point of the parable becomes clear only when we notice that there is something unexpected about the way in which Jesus applies it (verse 36). One would have expected the application to run something like this: 'The Samaritan recognized the victim of the robbers as his neighbour without having to be told. Be like him and know that those who need your help are your neighbours.' But, although Jesus does say in verse 37, 'Go, and do thou likewise', He comes to this application in a curiously roundabout way. This difficulty, however, so far from being a reason for concluding (as some do) that the present setting of the parable is secondary, is the clue to the parable's real meaning.

Jesus does not give the lawyer a direct answer, because his question is a bad question. Even a pagan could know who is his neighbour without being told. The Latin poet Terence had written in the second century B.C. the famous line: 'I am a man: nothing human do I count foreign to myself' (*Homo sum: humani nil a me alienum puto*). How much more might a member of the people of God be expected to recognize his neighbour in his fellow-man as such – and most of all one whose job it is to study and to teach the law! For such a man to ask who is his neighbour is to betray the fact that he has a hard and loveless heart. It can only be an attempt to excuse himself (cf. 'desiring to justify himself' in verse 29) for evasions of his responsibility. It has the same sort of ring as Cain's cynical question: 'Am I my brother's keeper?' (Genesis 4.9). For the man who sincerely wishes to love his neighbour the real problem is not to know who is his neighbour but to know how to be able to love him.

Jesus by asking, 'Which of these three, thinkest thou, proved neighbour unto him that fell among the robbers?', turns the whole matter upside down, as it were, or rather sets the right way up what the lawyer is seeing upside down. Thereby He not only indicates that 'it is love that is fundamental, not neighbourhood' (T. W. Manson), but also does something more. He invites the lawyer, in the first place, not to ask himself whether he is going to be like the priest or the Levite or the Samaritan (not, in other words, to think of himself as someone in a position generously to show mercy to his neighbour), but rather to see himself in the situation of the man needing help. To do this would be to let in a flood of light both on the question, 'Who is my neighbour?' and also – compare Matthew 7.12 – on the question: 'What does it mean to love my neighbour as myself?'

Moreover, on a deeper level the lawyer *is* needy – before God. And if he can be brought to realize – what, as a student and a teacher of God's law, he has no excuse for not realizing – his need of God's mercy, his inability to justify himself before God, he will be on the way to learning his duty to his neighbour. We may compare 2 Chronicles 28.10 ('. . . are there not even with you trespasses of your own against the LORD your God?') and its sequel, and also Isabella's words to Angelo in *Measure for Measure*:

> 'How would you be,
> If He, which is the top of judgment, should
> But judge you as you are? O! think on that,
> And mercy then will breathe within your lips,
> Like man new made.'

But the man in the parable with whom the lawyer is invited to identify himself was not only in grievous need; he also received mercy and succour. And what about the lawyer? Is he not himself the recipient of God's mercy? Does he not remember the words, 'Bless the LORD, O my soul, And forget not all his benefits: Who forgiveth all thine iniquities; Who healeth all thy diseases; Who redeemeth thy life from destruction; Who crowneth thee with lovingkindness and tender mercies . . .'? Could he but realize a little of his own indebtedness to God, he would find not only that he recognized his neighbour but also that he was able to make a beginning of loving him as himself.

But there is still more to be said. In the two verses immediately preceding this pericope we read: 'And turning to the disciples, he said privately, Blessed are the eyes which see the things that ye see: for I say unto you, that many prophets and kings desired to see the things which ye see, and saw them not; and to hear the things which ye hear, and heard them not' (Luke 10.23–24). Had the lawyer's eyes only been able to see and his ears to hear, he might have recognized the One who was talking to him. The signs of the kingdom of God were to be seen: 'the blind receive their sight, and the lame walk, the lepers are cleansed, and the deaf hear, and the dead are raised up, and the poor have good tidings preached to them' (Matthew 11.5). God had visited His people. In the person of Jesus He had actually come where such poor sinners as this loveless lawyer were in their lostness and need. Though C. H. Dodd was right in objecting to Augustine's allegorical interpretation of this parable, there is real truth in Augustine's identification of the Samaritan with Jesus Christ. (The parable of the Good Samaritan is surely a parable of the Kingdom of God, in spite of the fact that it is not one of the parables dealt with at length by Dodd in his book, *The Parables of the Kingdom*). For us who know, not only what the lawyer did not recognize, but also what he could not know – the cost at which the Son of God came where we were and bound up our wounds – this is the very heart of the parable's message. It reminds us of Him. And those, who remember that in their deep need they have received mercy at Christ's hands and that it is by His mercy alone that they live moment by moment, cannot help but be grateful and, in their gratitude to Christ, have their hearts opened toward their neighbours. And when we remember too that Christ has not only been our good neighbour who has succoured us at immeasurable cost but is also to be recognized in those who need our aid, we can accept the command to go and do likewise (verse 37) not just as a command to be obeyed but as a gracious gift.

We have now seen what is the heart of the message of this parable; but there remains something else which should be mentioned. This pericope is a very special warning to the theologian. The lawyer is a professional theologian and can give a perfect theological answer – 'Thou hast answered right', says Jesus – and yet he can ask: 'Who is my neighbour?' How easy it is for the theologian, when faced by an essentially simple moral challenge, to discover endless complications behind which to hide from the necessity of making a decision of love and acting upon it! How easy to have a vast academic knowledge of the Bible and God and theology, and yet to fail to recognize the occasion which calls us to do that about which we are continually talking!

There are also the priest and the Levite in the parable. We are perhaps meant to understand that they were returning home after a period of Temple-duty. They are a frightening reminder that it is possible to be so preoccupied with our theological, religious, and ecclesiastical concerns, that we have no time or energy left for the neighbour who needs our help – and so none for Christ Himself. It is scarcely possible to imagine more pathetic figures than the theologian who is so busy writing books (perhaps even about New Testament ethics) and the ecclesiastical statesman who is so busy with church politics, that they have no time to bother about those social and political issues in which justice and mercy and truth are at stake, and so, like the priest and the Levite, pass by on the other side, thereby showing that their theology and their church statesmanship are all the time not for the glory of God but for their own glory.

2

THE WATCHMAN

And the word of the LORD came unto me, saying,
Son of man, speak to the children of thy people, and
say unto them, When I bring the sword upon a land,
if the people of the land take a man from among
them, and set him for their watchman: if, when he
seeth the sword come upon the land, he blow the
trumpet, and warn the people; then whosoever
heareth the sound of the trumpet, and taketh not
warning, if the sword come, and take him away, his
blood shall be upon his own head. He heard the
sound of the trumpet, and took not warning; his
blood shall be upon him: whereas if he had taken
warning he should have delivered his soul. But if the
watchman see the sword come, and blow not the
trumpet, and the people be not warned, and the
sword come, and take any person from among them;
he is taken away in his iniquity, but his blood will I
require at the watchman's hand. So thou, son of
man, I have set thee a watchman unto the house of
Israel; therefore hear the word at my mouth, and
give them warning from me. When I say unto the
wicked, O wicked man, thou shalt surely die, and
thou dost not speak to warn the wicked from his
way; that wicked man shall die in his iniquity, but his
blood will I require at thine hand. Nevertheless, if
thou warn the wicked of his way to turn from it, and
he turn not from his way; he shall die in his iniquity,
but thou hast delivered thy soul.

And thou, son of man, say unto the house of

Israel: Thus ye speak, saying, Our transgressions and our sins are upon us, and we pine away in them; how then should we live? Say unto them, As I live, saith the Lord GOD, I have no pleasure in the death of the wicked; but that the wicked turn from his way and live: turn ye, turn ye from your evil ways; for why will ye die, O house of Israel? And thou, son of man, say unto the children of thy people, The righteousness of the righteous shall not deliver him in the day of his transgression; and as for the wickedness of the wicked, he shall not fall thereby in the day that he turneth from his wickedness: neither shall he that is righteous be able to live thereby in the day that he sinneth. When I say to the righteous, that he shall surely live; if he trust to his righteousness, and commit iniquity, none of his righteous deeds shall be remembered; but in his iniquity that he hath committed, therein shall he die. Again, when I say unto the wicked, Thou shalt surely die; if he turn from his sin, and do that which is lawful and right; if the wicked restore the pledge, give again that he had taken by robbery, walk in the statutes of life, committing no iniquity; he shall surely live, he shall not die. None of his sins that he hath committed shall be remembered against him: he hath done that which is lawful and right; he shall surely live.

(Ezekiel 33.1–16.)

Ezekiel, the priest, the son of Buzi, was among those Jews whom Nebuchadrezzar deported to Babylonia in 597 B.C. along with King Jehoiachin; and he exercised his ministry among the exiles from 593 to 571 B.C. The book which bears his name falls naturally into two parts which correspond with the two periods of his prophetic ministry. The turning-point was the arrival of the news that Jerusalem had been destroyed (586 B.C.). The theme of the first twenty-four chapters is the certainty that Jerusalem is going to be destroyed – the sins of the people make it necessary, since God is God. The message of the remaining twenty-four chapters is one of restoration and renewal. The passage with which we are concerned falls in the second half of the book and so belongs to the second period of the prophet's ministry.

I

The first six verses give the illustration of the watchman. In time of danger the need for a watchman is obvious. When the enemy may attack at any moment, there must always be someone on the look-out, lest the citizens be taken by surprise. And if, when the enemy approaches, and the watchman sounds the alarm, some hear the alarm and yet do not act upon it, if they lose their lives, their blood will be on their own heads – the watchman is not to blame. But should the watchman fail to sound the alarm when he sees the enemy approaching, then the blood of the citizens who lose their lives will be upon the watchman's head.

In verses 7–9 we get the application of this to the prophet's ministry. God has set him as a watchman for Israel. (Here paradoxically it is actually the 'enemy' himself who appoints the watchman to warn the people of his approach!) The prophet's task is to watch for God's word, and, when he hears it, to warn the people from God. And, as with the watchman of verses 1–6, if the prophet faithfully fulfils his duty, then, if the wicked man does not heed the warning, his blood will be on his own head, and the prophet will have delivered his own soul; but, if the prophet fails to give the warning, God will hold him responsible for the death of the wicked – 'his blood will I require at thine hand' (verse 8).

That this whole passage bears directly on the task of the Christian minister in relation to his congregation is obvious. It reminds us that he is set by God as a watchman for his congregation to watch diligently on their behalf for God's Word and, as he hears it, faithfully to communicate it, in its fullness and in its concrete particularity, not only to the congregation as a whole, but also to the individual members severally. And the latter half of verse 8 leave us in no doubt about the minister's accountability to God for those whom God has committed to his care.

But what is said here may also be applied to the ministry of the congregation as a whole in relation to the community in which it is set, and also – though we should never forget the difference between the people of Israel and all other nations – to the ministry of the whole church within a particular country in relation to the nation. And it is this application which we are to consider more fully here.

What then does it mean that the church is set by God as a watchman on behalf of the community? It means that the primary business of the church – of the church as a whole, not just of the clergy – is to hear the Word of God. And, since we are to hear the Word of God not only as God's message addressed to ourselves but also as the message we in turn have to pass on, it is doubly necessary for us to strive after clarity of understanding. We cannot hope to proclaim clearly and convincingly something which remains for ourselves indistinct and vague. The church which is going to fulfil its watchman function faithfully will be a church which is prepared to wrestle with Holy Scripture, not one that is lazy of mind, and content with hazy notions and vague sentiments.

It means also that we have to hear the Word of God not just in its bearing upon our own lives and the life of the church, but also in its bearing on the lives of our non-Christian neighbours and on the life of the nation – a task we cannot possibly fulfil without a real understanding of the situation of our neighbours, their problems, fears and interests, their joys and sorrows, and a real understanding of the various social and political issues of our time. God's watchman on behalf of the community must constantly study not only the Bible but also the daily newspaper.

But the watchman has not only to watch for the approach of the enemy, he has also to sound the alarm. The prophet Ezekiel was not only to watch for God's Word on behalf of Israel, he was also, as he heard it, to communicate it to the people. So too the church has not only to hear the Word of God on behalf of the community, but also to bring it effectively to the community. In this task of communication the problem is not just one of catching the attention of the public. If this were all, it would not be very difficult. An unusual and superlatively expensive new church building or a clergyman denying the doctrines which even the man-in-the-street knows he has solemnly promised to teach is enough to cause a sensation. And it is only to be expected that something as bizarre as a theologian propounding what seems to amount to Christianity without God will hit the headlines. It is also to be expected that some of the clergy will hail it as a break-through, an outstanding success in communication. But the communication to which we are called is not just a matter of making our voice heard; it is also a matter of communicating the message with which we have been entrusted by God. The church has not succeeded in communication just because it has attracted public attention: it only succeeds in communication when it brings effectively to men's minds and hearts the authentic message of the living God, the Father of our Lord Jesus Christ.

But the communication of God's Word is a costly business. We may see something of its costliness for Ezekiel in chapter 24, verses 15–24, where he tells us how God warned him that his wife, whom he clearly loved very dearly, was going to die, but forbade him to weep or to show any outward signs of mourning. He might 'Sigh, but not aloud'; for his strange behaviour in his bereavement was to be a sign to the people of Israel to bring home to them the dreadfulness of the judgment that was still to come upon them. So the prophet had to be selfless and self-forgetting, subordinating even his deep personal grief to the service of the people whom God had appointed him to serve.

The costliness we are called to reckon with is not the alleged need to rid the Christian message of all those elements which modern man, who is said to have 'come of age', finds difficult to accept. (This bright new idea is after all as old as the first century A.D. We may think, for example, of the false teachers to whom the First Epistle of John refers. They too were ready to throw out the gospel in order to make Christianity acceptable to 'the modern mind'.) It is rather a matter of allowing our lives and the life of the church as a whole to be purged of those things which are flagrantly inconsistent with the gospel we profess to believe, a matter of readiness for self-sacrifice, of sincerity and honesty, of self-forgetting humble service of the community, and especially of the needy, the weak and the unwanted. The cost of communication is the cost of real love for those to whom God's message is to be communicated – a love which will force the church's life to be turned outward in mission and ministry, instead of being turned inward in preoccupation with its own self-preservation and the promotion of its own vested interests. And real love will often involve suffering and anguish (compare Exodus 32.32, Romans 9.3).

And the watchman's duty involves haste. The alarm must be sounded effectively before the enemy is upon the city. Each moment is precious. So it is also with the church's ministry to the community in which it is placed. How much we need to recover the biblical sense of urgency, which can wing the preacher's word and enable the church to act with energy, decisiveness and courage, and which, since it is rooted in the gospel itself, is something altogether different from the restlessness and fussiness of a church which has largely lost its nerve because it has lost its grip on the gospel and is being tossed hither and thither at the mercy of every gust of false doctrine!

II

In verses 1–9 attention was concentrated on the responsibility of the watchman. Only a part of one verse (verse 5) referred to the possibility of the alarm's being heeded, and even there the reference is in the form of an unfulfilled conditional sentence! But all the way through these verses it was, of course, implied that the purpose of the appointment of the watchman was that those whose lives were threatened by danger might heed his warning and be saved. Now in verses 10–16 what was implicit in the previous section is made explicit. To the despondent question of the people of Israel, 'Our transgressions and our sins are upon us, and we pine away in them; how then should we live?' (verse 10), the prophet is told to answer: 'As I live, saith the Lord GOD, I have no pleasure in the death of the wicked; but that the wicked turn from his way and live: turn ye, turn ye from your evil ways; for why will ye die, O house of Israel?' (verse 11).

Ezekiel's ministry to his people was to be fulfilled in the knowledge that God takes no pleasure in the death of the wicked but desires their repentance and salvation. And here we have to remember something which Ezekiel could not know – that the measure of God's desire for the repentance and salvation of the wicked is the cross of Jesus Christ, His dear Son. The congregation's mission to the local community and the church's mission to the nation in which it is set must be based upon this certainty. We must not for a moment lose sight of the fact that God wills the salvation of those to whom we are sent.

And yet are we not often tempted to lose sight of this? How easily, and without our realizing it, does contempt creep into our denunciation of the deeds of the wicked – a contempt which is not only contempt for their thoughts and ways, but also contempt of their persons! When we think about those who are busy corrupting the life of our nation, those who deliberately encourage vice in others so that they may make money out of it, or those politicians who make all their appeal to men's selfishness, or when we think of the crass irresponsibility and thoughtless selfishness of so many of our countrymen, it is desperately easy to give way to such a feeling of contempt; and the more real our patriotism, the greater the temptation is. But if the church in a nation is faithfully to fulfil its watchman function, it has got to remember that the basest and the most degenerate are people for whom Christ died, people in whose death God takes no pleasure, but whom He desires to save. Though we ought indeed to call depravity depravity, whether in high or low, and to hate other people's sins as well as our own, we dare not, if we would be faithful to our task, despise persons, for whom Christ died. And we must not be like Jonah, resentful of God's patience with the wicked, or like those who in the not very distant past took it ill that some of the war criminals of the Nuremberg trials were converted and partook of the Lord's Supper. We cannot remind ourselves often enough that Christ died even for the most unscrupulous politician and for all others who mislead and corrupt their fellow-men.

In our mission as God's watchman on behalf of the community we must ever cherish hope in our hearts for the unbeliever, refusing to take him altogether seriously in his unbelief. A church which had ceased to have a sober Christian hope for all those to whom it was sent could no longer be a faithful watchman of God on their behalf.

III

There is also another note sounded in the course of verses 10–16. Verses 12 and 13 contain these words: 'The righteousness of the righteous shall not deliver him in the day of his transgression ... neither shall he that is righteous be able to live thereby in the day that he sinneth. When I say to the righteous, that he shall surely live; if he trust to his righteousness, and commit iniquity, none of his righteous deeds shall be remembered; but in his iniquity that he hath committed, therein shall he die.' We may receive them as a reminder that the church must not seek to fulfil its function as a watchman in a spirit of self-righteousness and complacency but rather in a humble and chastened spirit, in the knowledge that it too is under the judgment of the gospel, and lives not by its own righteousness but by God's mercy in Jesus Christ, a warning to us to speak to our neighbours and to our countrymen as fellow-sinners, who have ever to be on our guard lest by any means, after that we have preached to others, we ourselves should be rejected.

3

DIAKONIA[1]

But when the Son of man shall come in his glory, and all the angels with him, then shall he sit on the throne of his glory: and before him shall be gathered all the nations: and he shall separate them one from another, as the shepherd separateth the sheep from the goats: and he shall set the sheep on his right hand, but the goats on the left. Then shall the King say unto them on his right hand, Come, ye blessed of my Father, inherit the kingdom prepared for you from the foundation of the world: for I was an hungred, and ye gave me meat: I was thirsty, and ye gave me drink: I was a stranger, and ye took me in; naked, and ye clothed me: I was sick, and ye visited me: I was in prison, and ye came unto me. Then shall the righteous answer him, saying, Lord, when saw we thee an hungred, and fed thee? or athirst, and gave thee drink? And when saw we thee a stranger, and took thee in? or naked, and clothed thee? And when saw we thee sick, or in prison, and came unto thee? And the King shall answer and say unto them, Verily I say unto you, Inasmuch as ye did it unto one of these my brethren, *even* these last, ye did it unto me. Then shall he say also unto them on the left hand, Depart from me, ye cursed, into the eternal fire which is prepared for the devil and his angels: for I was an hungred, and ye gave me no meat: I was thirsty, and ye gave me no drink: I was a stranger,

[1] Preached before the University of Cambridge on 5 February 1961.

and ye took me not in; naked, and ye clothed me not; sick, and in prison, and ye visited me not. Then shall they also answer, saying, Lord, when saw we thee an hungred, or athirst, or a stranger, or naked, or sick, or in prison, and did not minister unto thee? Then shall he answer them, saying, Verily I say unto you, Inasmuch, as ye did it not unto one of these least, ye did it not unto me, And these shall go away into eternal punishment: but the righteous into eternal life.

(Matthew 25.31–46.)

I am not going to attempt in the space of a single sermon to indicate even in outline all the treasures of this peculiarly rich and suggestive passage. I shall only try to draw out some of the things which it has to say to us.

I hope I may be forgiven if I begin by saying something (necessarily a little bit complicated) about two exegetical questions, which are of vital importance for the interpretation of the passage as a whole. They are: (i) Who are meant by 'all the nations' in verse 32 ('and before him shall be gathered all the nations . . .')? and (ii) Who are meant by 'these my brethren, even these least' in verse 40 ('Inasmuch as ye did it unto one of these my brethren, even these least, ye did it unto me') and the similar 'these least' in verse 45?

With regard to the first of these questions, the conceivable meanings of 'all the nations' are: first, all the Gentiles, as opposed to Jews; second, all the heathen, as opposed to the disciples of Jesus, the Christian Church, so including the non-believing Jews; and, third, all men, including the disciples of Jesus. Of these, although the first and the second have recently been favoured by some New Testament scholars, the last is, I think, the only one that is really possible. For the passage as it stands is surely to be understood as a solemn appeal and warning to those who are being addressed, an appeal to them to be the sort of people who will at the last be counted righteous and a warning to them not to be the sort of people who at the last will be rejected. If that is so, it follows that the people whom Jesus is addressing are intended to see themselves as included among those who are going to be judged; in other words, they must be included under the term 'all the nations'. And it is clear that the evangelist, at any rate, understood this discourse as having been addressed to the disciples; for he has made it the last section and climax of a great block of teaching which he specifically represents as being addressed to the disciples 'privately'. For Matthew, at any rate, then, I think 'all the nations' meant 'all men', including Christians. And, while it certainly seems to be true that the evangelists have sometimes applied to the Church teaching which was not originally addressed to disciples, it is, I think, extraordinarily difficult to imagine circumstances in the ministry of Jesus in which He is likely to have addressed anything like this present discourse to anyone other than His disciples. So I would conclude that, if this particular phrase goes back to our Lord Himself – and I see no reason why it should not – then for Him as for Matthew 'all the nations' included His disciples.

The second question can, fortunately, be answered much more briefly. Of the two conceivable meanings of 'these my brethren, even these least' – on the one hand, disciples in need, and, on the other hand, the needy generally, irrespective of whether they are Christ's disciples or not – although some scholars have recently favoured the former meaning, the latter is surely the only one that is really possible; for, while all the individuals denoted by 'all the nations' (whichever sense we give it) would be sure to have had some opportunity to succour a fellow-man in need, it is obvious that they certainly could not all be assumed to have had a chance to succour a needy Christian. Thus, if 'these my brethren, even these least' referred only to Christians, such a succouring or not succouring could not possibly be a universally applicable criterion.

We conclude then that this passage refers not to a judgment either of the Gentiles or of all non-Christians, according to their treatment of Christians in need or of their needy fellow-men generally, but to a judgment of all men, including Christians, according to their treatment of their needy fellow-men, irrespective of whether these are Christians or not.

It is now high time to ask: What are some of the things which this passage has to say to us?

In the first place, it directs our attention to *the future* – to the time when He, who in His earthly ministry was the lowly and suffering Son of man, and who even now that He is at the right hand of the Father, exalted and reigning, the One to whom all authority has already been given in heaven and on earth, the ruler of the kings of the earth, is still not yet manifested as King, shall at last be seen to be King. (Notice how He who in verse 31 is spoken of as 'Son of man' is in verse 34 referred to as 'the King'.) It points to the Parousia, the glorious second coming of Christ, the end of history. At the very moment that Jesus is about to face His bitterest and most extreme humiliation, His arrest, trial and death as a malefactor, He looks forward with unshaken confidence to the moment of His final and unambiguous manifestation as King of all.

But this manifestation of Jesus Christ as King will mean for us men the final judgment. When He comes again with glory, it will be to judge both the quick and dead: '. . . then shall he sit on the throne of his glory: and before him shall be gathered all the nations: and he shall separate them one from another, as the shepherd separateth the sheep from the goats . . .'. The passage we are considering, though often referred to as the Parable of the Sheep and the Goats, is not so much a parable as a straight discourse, a sermon – if you like – about the final judgment. The illustration of the shepherd and his sheep and goats takes only one and a half verses. Its purpose is simply to indicate how easily and unhesitatingly Christ will carry out the final division of men. The shepherd has no difficulty in distinguishing the sheep from the goats; he can tell the one from the other at a glance. So swift and sure will be the division of men by Christ in the last judgment.

The passage is impressive not only for its moral grandeur and deep earnestness, but also for its restraint and sobriety. Here are no vivid colours, no picturesque details, nothing of the bizarre fantasy characteristic of Jewish apocalyptic. In its restraint and sobriety, its seriousness and earnestness, this passage reminds us of something which much of our present-day British Christianity in its easy-going superficiality tends to ignore. It reminds us that the all-important question for each one of us is: What will the King have to say to us when at the last we appear before Him? Shall we be among those to whom He will say, 'Come, ye blessed of my Father, inherit the kingdom prepared for you from the foundation of the world', or among those to whom He will say, 'Depart from me, ye cursed . . .'?

And do not let us fail to see that in thus asserting so earnestly the ultimate accountability of each individual for himself, our Lord has given to the individual man the

101

charter of his inalienable dignity. The man who knows that at the last he will have to answer before Christ the King for the use he has made of his life and his opportunities, and that he will not then be able to shrug off his responsibility upon others, knows also his own human dignity. Here is reason for standing erect in the face of coercion, for being a real man and not a mere conforming shadow, for refusing to yield either to a tyrant's tortures or the inanity of a society dominated by such things as hidden persuaders and the craze for status and prestige.

But, in the second place, this passage drives us back relentlessly to *the present*. Here is no apocalypse such as might gratify idle curiosity or foster a smug assurance. Jesus gives His disciples no encouragement to indulge in fanciful speculation about the future. Rather He directs their attention back to the present. For it is in the present that their eternal destiny is being decided. It is here and now in this life that we encounter our fellow-men in their need and wretchedness, the hungry and the thirsty, the strangers, the naked, the sick and the prisoners, and can minister to them – or neglect to do so. In this judgment scene, sketched with such simplicity and restraint, everything is represented as depending on whether or not men have in their lifetime shown compassion to their fellow-men in distress.

Judgment according to works this certainly is, but not in any legalistic sense. It is not said here that the righteous have earned their reward, that their deeds of mercy are meritorious works for which they deserve everlasting life. It may perhaps be fair to argue, as some commentators have done, that the very fact that the King bids them inherit the kingdom prepared for them from the foundation of the world points back behind their actions to the undeserved grace of God. But, however that may be, we must surely understand this passage in the light of the rest of our Lord's teaching. Elsewhere Jesus says to His disciples: 'When ye shall have done all the things that are commanded you, say, We are unprofitable servants; we have done that which it was our duty to do'. So I take it that in this passage the righteous are not thought of as having put the King under an obligation to themselves by their works of mercy, but rather simply as having shown by their works the reality of their faith. We can never by feeding the hungry, clothing the naked, and other such actions, earn our salvation; but, if we truly believe in Jesus Christ, if we have any real faith at all, we cannot help but begin to be open to the need and distress of our neighbours. The presence of such openness may be evidence of a genuine faith; its absence is a conclusive proof that any faith we profess to have is merely counterfeit.

But Jesus is here not only bringing home to His disciples the decisive importance of the present and the fact that in the final judgment men will be divided according to whether or not they have in this life shown compassion to their needy fellow-men. He is also disclosing a mystery to them. In this judgment scene those who think that they are meeting their Judge for the first time learn that they have actually been meeting Him during the whole course of their lives – without recognizing Him. For us it is the secret that in the present time the Lord Jesus Christ is not only at the right hand of the Father, but also comes to us again and again not only in the Word and Sacraments, but also in the flesh and blood of our fellow-men in their need and distress – in the flesh and blood of individual men and women and children in their wretchedness. To say that they are His ambassadors and that therefore

103

what we do or omit to do to them is counted as done or not done to Him does not, I think, exhaust the meaning of what is said here. Something more than this would seem to be intended – namely, that there is a real presence of the exalted Christ in the persons of His brethren in their need and distress comparable with His real presence in the Word and Sacraments, that as truly as He is present mysteriously and hiddenly, in His freedom and lordship, in the Holy Scriptures read and heard, by means of broken human words, and in the Holy Supper by means of bread and wine, so truly is He present mysteriously and hiddenly, in His freedom and lordship, in our daily life by means of our fellow-men who need our assistance.

This presence of the King in the persons of the least of His brethren is indeed a mystery, which the world as a whole will not know till the final judgment takes place. But, although Jesus in this judgment scene represents the righteous as well as the unrighteous as not having recognized who it was with whom they were dealing, it is perfectly clear that He does not want the mystery to be hidden from His disciples. The whole purpose of this discourse on the final judgment is to reveal the mystery to them. He is preparing them for the time when He will have left them – for the time between His departure and His coming again in glory. That time is to be filled by His disciples with a loving ministering to Him in the persons of His needy brethren.

To know this mystery is to know that in our service of the needy all thought of patronizing is once and for all excluded. How could we feel ourselves superior to those who come to us clothed with the majesty of Christ Himself, as persons who are His ambassadors, or rather whose suffering flesh veils His mysterious presence? To the world they may seem to be in the position of beggars who must humbly crave our favour; but the eye of faith sees in them the Lord Jesus Christ, who comes to claim that which is His by right. They have an absolute right to our service in virtue of His decision to be thanked and loved in them.

To know this mystery is, further, to be set free to serve our fellow-men in their need with joy and thankfulness. For, seeing that our debt to Christ is so great that we can never cease to be His debtors, how could we not welcome the persons of His needy brethren with joy and thankfulness as His gracious gift to us of the opportunity to love and serve and thank Him? Eloquently does John Calvin sum up what this passage has to say to us about the present in his comment on verse 40:

> We must be prodigiously insensitive, if compassion be not drawn from our bowels by this statement, that Christ is either neglected or honoured in the persons of those who need our assistance. So then, when we are reluctant to assist the poor, may the Son of God come before our eyes, to whom to refuse anything is a monstrous sacrilege.

I come now to the third, and last, part of my sermon. That all this applies to us as individuals is obvious, and I am not going to labour the point. Most of you, no doubt, are as aware as I am of the bitter need of our times, of the thirty to forty millions of refugees, of the two-thirds of the world's population either seriously under-nourished or actually starving, of the multitudes who suffer preventable disease for lack of medical supplies and care. You will have read, as I have, of Algerian children trying to relieve their hunger by eating earth, of people dying of starvation in the Congo, of famine in China, of the desperate continuing poverty of India. And it is unlikely that there is anyone here who is quite indifferent to all this human suffering. Many of you, no doubt, will already have been generous in your response to the various humanitarian appeals. With regard to this personal, individual aspect I shall do no more than simply put into words one question which seems to me to arise naturally at this point. It is this: Does not the amount that we give for the relief of our fellow-human beings, when we look at it again in the light of the passage which we have been considering and in that light compare it with what we spend on our comforts and luxuries and pleasures, begin to look rather less generous – perhaps even paltry and mean?

But there is another aspect, about which I want to speak in the remaining minutes. It seems to me that this passage, as well as putting urgent questions to us about our lives as individuals, has some very important things to say to us about the corporate life of the Church.

It is not without significance that the verb (translated 'minister' in our Bible) which is used in verse 44 as a general term to cover all the various services to the needy which the King has mentioned is the verb *diakonein* ('Lord, when saw we thee an hungred, or athirst, or a stranger, or naked, or sick, or in prison, and did not minister unto thee?'); for this verb, together with its cognates, has had a special importance in the Church's life and thought. These words are quite often used in the New Testament in their original connotation – that is, with reference to waiting at table; they are also used generally of Christ's service of men, and of men's service of Christ and of God; but they are most characteristically used with reference to the loving, practical service of the needy and afflicted and the administration of the material resources of the Christian community. The noun *diakonos* (which we have in English in the form 'deacon') came to be used especially of those ministers of the early Church whose function it was to be the agents of the Church's charitable work and to administer its funds, and the abstract noun *diakonia* denotes especially that sort of ministry.

It seems to me that the first thing which our text has to say to us here is that *diakonia*, the service of the needy and afflicted, ought to be of central importance in the life of every congregation. If the mystery which this text reveals is really true, if Christ Himself is really present in the persons of the least of His brethren, then to minister to Him in their persons cannot be only a matter for Christians as individuals; it must also be an essential and important part of the corporate life of the Christian community. To suppose that the Lord Jesus Christ is pleased with a congregation's public worship, however beautifully and solemnly it be executed, if the congregation is all the time neglecting Him as He comes to it in the persons of the distressed, is clearly illusion. And a collection every now and then for charitable purposes hardly measures up to what is required. What our text suggests is surely rather a diligent and continual service, a never ceasing to be on the watch for opportunities to serve the afflicted.

But for this imagination is necessary. Times change, and new forms of service have to take the place of old. It is true that a welfare State such as our own does much of the humanitarian work which the Church used to do; but the assumption that all that needs to be done for the weak, the handicapped, and the misfits of society is being done, however agreeable it may be to the complacency of the well-established, is, of course, untrue. For, in spite of all that the State does – and Christians should certainly be glad that it does so much – there remains a vast amount of human distress close to our doors. I mention just one example – the plight of the discharged prisoner, who steps out from prison often with no home to go to and with only a few shillings in his pocket, to start seeking a job in a society which not unnaturally is suspicious of ex-prisoners, often to find that, as soon as his immediate past is known, the doors of opportunity shut in his face. It is hardly surprising that very many ex-prisoners are back in jail within a few weeks of being discharged. Had our churches been awake, many a congregation or local council of churches would surely by now have established its own small family-type hostel for discharged prisoners (on the lines of the few which are in existence), where the ex-prisoner might have been given that sense of belonging, of being loved, the absence of which may well have been the root cause of his anti-social behaviour. And lists of members willing to employ ex-prisoners could have been compiled, or, at the least, much more help could have been given to the voluntary society which tries with inadequate funds to do something for discharged prisoners. Many other examples of need close at hand will suggest themselves, wherever a living congregation understands the meaning of *diakonia*.

But at the present time the greatest need and the greatest opportunities for service undoubtedly lie farther afield, among the refugees and in the under-developed territories. Alas for the congregation which is so parochial in its vision as to feel that its opportunities for *diakonia* are less today than they used to be and not to realize that they have in fact been multiplied many thousand times by modern means of communication and transport!

Secondly, it seems to me that this text raises for us the question of the diaconate. Admittedly the important thing is that *diakonia* should be practised in, and by, every congregation and parish, and it certainly can be practised even where there are no office-bearers charged with a special responsibility for it. A congregation does not necessarily fail to serve the needy because it has no deacons. But may it not be that, where the office of deacon has been discontinued or has been transformed into something quite different from what it was in the first few centuries, it is more easy for the function of *diakonia* itself to be neglected? And may not the fact that in some churches the diaconate has become merely a stage on the way to the priesthood, while in others it has become wholly concerned with ministers' stipends and the upkeep of church buildings, point to the presence of a very real element of disorder in our church life? Perhaps in our present preoccupation with questions of Presbyterians and Methodists taking episcopacy into their systems, and Anglicans taking the eldership into theirs, we have given less attention than we should have done to the question of deacons. Does not our text at least raise the question whether it may not be quite as important for all the churches in Britain to consider seriously taking into their systems a diaconate primarily concerned with ministering to Christ in the persons of the needy, such as the New Testament diaconate seems, despite opinions to the contrary, to have been, as it is for some of them to consider taking episcopacy, and others the eldership, into their systems?

Thirdly, and finally, the mystery of Christ's presence in all who are needy and wretched cannot be irrelevant to the realm of ecclesiastical finance. The disturbing questions which our text raises here and the need for a radical,

theological rethinking of the whole business of the
Church's management of its material resources which it
discloses can, I think, hardly be more vividly suggested
than by a quotation from St Ambrose's *de officiis
ministrorum*. His defence of himself against those who
had reproached him for having broken up sacred vessels
for the ransom of prisoners includes these sentences:

> The Church has gold not to hoard but to
> distribute and to succour those in need . . . Would
> not the Lord say, Why have you allowed so many
> poor to die of hunger? You certainly had gold, with
> which to have ministered to their sustenance. Why
> have so many captives been taken away for sale and
> not redeemed? . . . It had been better to preserve
> living than metallic vessels. These charges you will
> not be able to answer. For what would you say – I
> feared that the temple of God would lack ornament?
> He would answer: Sacraments require not gold; and
> things which are not bought with gold do not satisfy
> by gold. The ornament of the Sacraments is the
> redemption of captives.

Of course, the Church must spend a great deal of
money on the support of the clergy, the upkeep of church
buildings and many other things which are necessary if
the Church's mission is to be fulfilled. But our text would
seem to suggest that all proposed ecclesiastical
expenditure ought to be carefully scrutinized in the light
of the claims of human distress throughout the world, and
to call in question the use of the Church's money for
purposes of prestige, whether of one denomination over
against others, or of a congregation in the eyes of the local
community, or of the clergy. (And must we not admit that

much expenditure which purports to be to the greater glory of God is really for the sake of the prestige of men?) Does not our text also challenge us to ask ourselves very seriously whether there is not an essential truth in the conviction, which was held very strongly by some in the ancient Catholic Church and about which Calvin writes with such obvious warmth in one of the places in the *Institutes* where he is dealing with deacons, the conviction that the possessions of the Church are the patrimony of the poor, and whether for the Church to spend on frivolous or unnecessary purposes, or faithlessly to hoard, its resources, while the hungry starve, is not in fact a misappropriation of that which by right belongs to Christ in His needy ones, and therefore sacrilege?

May we as individuals, and may the whole Church in our country, understand the mystery which this passage discloses, and sincerely, gladly and lovingly minister to the Lord Jesus Christ in the persons of the least of His brethren.

4

THE GOSPEL IN ACTION[1]

And he said to him also that had bidden him, When thou makest a dinner or a supper, call not thy friends, nor thy brethren, nor thy kinsmen, nor rich neighbours; lest haply they also bid thee again, and a recompense be made thee. But when thou makest a feast, bid the poor, the maimed, the lame, the blind: and thou shalt be blessed; because they have not *wherewith* to recompense thee: for thou shalt be recompensed in the resurrection of the just.

(Luke 14.12–14.)

This is indeed a difficult passage. What Jesus is here recorded as saying seems a strange thing to say to one's host. While the positive command in verse 13 ('When thou makest a feast, bid the poor, the maimed, the lame, the blind') may perhaps strike us as rather idealistic and impracticable, the negative command in verse 12 ('When thou makest a dinner or a supper, call not thy friends, nor thy brethren, nor thy kinsmen, nor rich neighbours') seems, on the surface, to flout not merely social convention but courtesy itself and common decency. But we cannot be content simply to set the passage aside because it is difficult. It comes to us with the authority of Jesus, and so, as Christians, we have at least to try to discover what it means.

There is a technical point which it will be as well to notice right away. Whereas in English we can express a comparison conveniently and clearly, both the Hebrew of

[1] Preached in St Mary-le-Bow, Durham, on 4 November 1962.

112

the Old Testament and the Aramaic which our Lord spoke were deficient in this respect, and had to make do with not very satisfactory expedients. So, for instance, in Deuteronomy 21.15, the meaning is: 'If a man has two wives, and loves one more than the other . . .' but it is expressed by saying: 'If a man has two wives, the one beloved, and the other hated . . .'. Here 'hated' is used to express the idea of 'loved less', as it is also in Genesis 29.31, where it is not implied that Jacob actually hated Leah, but only that he loved her less than Rachel. Similar to this use of the opposite to express a lesser degree is the use of a negative, as when Hosea says in God's name: 'For I desire mercy, and not sacrifice' (Hosea 6.6), 'not desire' being used for 'desire less'. He does not mean that God does not want sacrifice at all, but that He wants it less than He wants mercy. Occasionally we get the same sort of thing in the New Testament, where the Greek reflects Aramaic idiom. So in Luke 14.26 Jesus says: 'If any man cometh unto me, and hateth not his own father, and mother, and wife, and children, and brethren, and sisters, yea, and his own life also, he cannot be my disciple.' Matthew 10.37 ('He that loveth father or mother more than me is not worthy of me; and he that loveth son or daughter more than me is not worthy of me') shows us how this must be understood. Now it is most probable that we should interpret the present passage along these lines – taking it to mean, not that a disciple of Jesus is never under any circumstances to entertain his friends or his relations, but that it is less important for him to do this than it is to entertain 'the poor, the maimed, the lame, the blind'. This eases the difficulty of the passage considerably; though it is still difficult, and we have still to discover the true significance of what Jesus is saying.

The clue to its meaning is the recognition that it has to

be seen against the background of Jesus' ministry. One of the things which provoked the opposition of the religious and respectable to Jesus was His association with those whom the Pharisees despised as 'sinners'. In Matthew 11.19 Jesus quotes the reproach that was being levelled against Him by His critics: 'a friend of publicans and sinners'. Much of our Lord's teaching was concerned with the defence of His ministry in the face of this criticism. The parable of the Prodigal Son (Luke 15.11–32) is one example of this. We have another in Mark 2.17. Jesus has accepted the hospitality of Levi, the tax-collector, whom He has called to be a disciple, and has been 'eating with the sinners and publicans'. The Scribes and the Pharisees have said to Jesus' disciples in scorn: 'He eateth and drinketh with publicans and sinners'; and Jesus when He hears about it says: 'They that are whole have no need of a physician, but they that are sick. I came not to call the righteous, but sinners'. It would be a strange doctor who refused to associate with the sick. And it is no more surprising that He who comes with God's message of mercy should be found among those who most obviously need God's mercy than it is that a doctor should be found among those who are ill.

So the words of our text are actually a vivid picture of the ministry of Jesus. This is how He Himself acted. He lavished His friendship on sinners. He deliberately associated with those who most obviously needed His help. As a matter of fact the whole, not just a part, of His ministry was of this nature; for in God's sight all men, even the most highly respectable, are sinners. He came into the world to serve and to save those who were in no position to recompense Him. This is the divine love. And this love is good news for us precisely because it is love of this nature – love for the unworthy. Every time we partake of the Lord's Supper we are reminded of the true character of God's love; for the Holy Supper is the meal for sinners. The Lord Jesus Christ invites to His Supper not His equals, nor His 'rich neighbours', but 'the poor, the maimed, the lame, the blind'. That is why we too may share in it.

When we see the passage, which we are trying to understand, against this background, it at once begins to make sense. If this is how Jesus Himself acted, if this is what the grace of God means, then it is not surprising that those who are Jesus' disciples should be summoned to behave according to this pattern. How else indeed should the Christian act but in such a way as to point to the grace of God by which he lives? The whole life of the Christian is meant to be a series of signs pointing to the reality of God's mercy in Jesus Christ.

What then is the significance of this passage for our personal lives? We have seen that Jesus most probably did not mean that we are never in any circumstances to show hospitality to our relatives, our friends, even our rich neighbours, but that it is much more important for us to show hospitality to the poor and needy. The reason why this is so is that to entertain one's friends and relations is simply human; our pagan neighbours do it just as much. Just as there is nothing specifically Christian in sitting down to one's dinner, in drinking when one is thirsty, or in going to bed for a night's sleep (though Christians should, of course, do these things in a Christian spirit of gratitude to God), so there is nothing characteristically Christian, nothing which particularly points to the grace of God in Jesus Christ, in showing hospitality to one's relatives and friends, one's colleagues, one's social equals or superiors. But when, for Christ's sake, because we know and understand what He has done for us men, we invite 'the poor, the maimed, the lame, the blind', then (though hospitality to the needy is, of course, not only shown by Christians) we do indeed set up pointers to God's grace in Jesus Christ.

So, while we shall not stop showing the ordinary hospitality to friends and equals, we are specially to make sure that we do this other thing. And, if we are busy people and if our resources are limited, we may well have to cut down our entertainment of those who are in a position to repay us like for like and possibly do what we do of it rather more frugally in order to have time and money for the more important thing.

And, when we do entertain 'the poor, the maimed, the lame, the blind', we shall have to beware of doing so in an ostentatious manner such as would in any way humiliate our guests. We must seek to treat them with the regard and reverence which are due to them as those in whom – according to Matthew 25.31–46 – the Lord Jesus Christ is Himself mysteriously present.

Let us just for a few moments think of some examples. To begin with, we may apply this to the matter of choosing our friends. In the light of this passage we may ask ourselves whether we should not sometimes offer our friendship to someone not because he has the same background as we do and shares the same interest and is personally congenial to us, but rather because he is lonely and needs a friend – and do it without any trace of patronizing.

And then there are the multitudes of the hungry in many parts of the world. In the light of this passage should we not regard it as more pressingly important that we should, by generous support of those organizations which are trying to do something to lessen this vast mass of suffering, show hospitality – albeit indirectly – to the hungry than that we should entertain those who without our hospitality would certainly not go short of food?

From among the many other examples of 'the poor, the maimed, the lame, the blind' in the sense of this passage, which may well occur to you if you begin seriously to look for them, I will single out just two groups of people who are sometimes overlooked. It is true that you may not be able to do very much for them while you are still students; but many of you will in a few years' time be in a position in which you could do something for some of them.

One group is the workers from overseas, from the West Indies, West Africa, Pakistan and elsewhere, who have settled in this country. It would be interesting and, I fear, humiliating for us as Christians to know how many of these neighbours of ours have never once been guests in an English home or even in a parish hall.

The other group which I want to mention is the people who find their way into prison. They, too, surely come within the category of 'the poor, the maimed, the lame, the blind'. There are various ways in which they may be helped. If, for instance, you should later on be living near a prison, you might offer yourselves for appointment as prison visitors. There are usually vacancies on the rolls of visitors – and Christian people ought surely to be eager to fill them; for the prison visitor, visiting the prisoners on his or her list regularly one by one, has a unique opportunity to offer friendship to people in sore need of it and to make them feel that there is someone who cares and is interested in them as persons. And, while the prisoner certainly needs help and friendship while he is 'inside', he often needs them even more on discharge. It is difficult for the respectable Church member to understand his feelings in the first few hours of freedom. The prison-gates open before him to freedom, but it is a freedom which for many an ex-prisoner is far from being friendly or inviting. The lucky ones have a relative to meet them, but many do not. In this city almost every weekday morning in the year, I suppose, some prisoners are discharged. I wonder how often one of the Christian citizens is there outside the gates to meet a discharged prisoner and take him home to breakfast, and then, perhaps, see him off at the station, getting his ticket for him to save him the embarrassment of handing in his warrant himself. And some of you will, in a few years' time, be employers. Perhaps you will think then of the weary and heartbreaking time which many a discharged prisoner experiences seeking a job – for many employers are unwilling to engage a man who has just come out of prison – and think too how rare a thing it is for an employer, because he is a Christian, to engage from time to time ex-prisoners, so giving them the chance to begin again – and yet how eloquently it may point to the gospel.

You will be able to think of many other examples of what this passage means in your own lives. It remains now just to notice very briefly that it has also a bearing on the corporate life of the Christian congregation. It reminds us that, while the social functions in which the members of a congregation enjoy one another's company may truly be an expression of their unity in the Lord – and it is indeed good and pleasant for brethren to dwell together in unity – a Christian congregation cannot stop here. If it did, it would be ceasing to be a Christian congregation and becoming a more, or less, religious club. The specially important thing, because the thing which most clearly points to the grace of God in Jesus Christ, is that the life of the congregation should be turned outward in humble and loving service of the suffering and needy of the world, of 'the poor, the maimed, the lame, the blind'.

5

MINISTER AND CONGREGATION IN THE LIGHT OF 2 CORINTHIANS 4.5–7

For we preach not ourselves, but Christ Jesus as Lord, and ourselves as your servants for Jesus' sake. Seeing it is God, that said, Light shall shine out of darkness, who shined in our hearts, to give the light of the knowledge of the glory of God in the face of Jesus Christ.

But we have this treasure in earthen vessels, that the exceeding greatness of the power may be of God, and not from ourselves. . . .

The apostle Paul here speaks of his own ministry, but in so doing he indicates the marks of every true ministry of the Word and the Sacraments.

1. *For we preach not ourselves* . . . Of the various temptations which beset the Christian minister, one of the chief and deadliest is the temptation to preach himself. It is an extremely insidious tendency, and none of us can claim that he has never yielded to it. It has many different forms and shapes. It can be highly refined and subtle as well as blatant and crude. Many of us are sensitive enough to recognize when a colleague succumbs at all obviously to it; but to notice when one yields to it oneself is very much harder. And usually when we succumb to it, we are quite unaware of what is happening.

This temptation besets the minister in the pulpit and in his study as he prepares his sermon. It is possible to

119

preach oneself quite blatantly, as, for example, when a preacher makes no really serious attempt at all to expound the Scriptures, offering to his congregation his own ideas, opinions, and prejudices. But more often the preaching of oneself is decently disguised and, indeed, unconscious – all the more dangerous because it is not at all obvious. There is the temptation to exploit the gospel, to exploit its drama, pathos, solemnity, and majesty, for the display of one's own powers, one's ability, eloquence, humour, learning, gifts of popular exposition. All unbeknown either to the congregation or the minister himself, the pulpit can become a platform for the minister's self-exhibition.

But this temptation is not limited to the sphere of preaching. It lurks at hand in all the minister's pastoral relationships. There is the constant temptation to build up the congregation and to build up individual personalities about one's own person. How often is that which is hailed as a successful ministry little more than success in winning a personal following! How easy it is to give way to the temptation to do one's work in such a way that the life of the congregation is everywhere dominated by the personality of the minister!

To this temptation every minister without exception yields to some extent. But the faithful minister resists it, and he prays to God earnestly for deliverance from it. To be aware of the existence of such a temptation and, still more, to be deeply conscious that one is oneself not free from it – these are great blessings.

Congregations are apt to put a stumbling-block in a minister's way, in relation to this temptation, and to encourage him to yield to it. For they are prone to like to be entertained and to enjoy a minister's self-exhibition. They are prone, too, to indulge in a personality cult. But this is the unkindest thing that a congregation has in its power to do to its pastor, for it tempts him to betray his ministry.

2. ... *but Christ Jesus* ... It is not ourselves, but Jesus Christ, the Man of Nazareth, the Son of God, to whom the Scriptures bear witness, whom we are called to preach. It is a good thing for the minister to ask himself about every sermon, 'Have I really preached Christ in this sermon?'. This does not mean, of course, that every sermon ought to be an 'evangelistic sermon' in the narrow sense. To preach Christ means preaching God's deed in Christ for the salvation of men in its fullness, God's gift of Himself to us, God's grace and mercy as gift, and also His claim to our allegiance. It is to preach the whole gospel – the whole counsel of God. The great events of the gospel should be central in our preaching, but they should be set forth in the context of the whole witness of Scripture to Christ. This will come about naturally only if the preacher preaches faithfully from the Bible. It is a good plan to preach steadily through a book of the Bible rather than to pick texts in accordance with one's own inclination; for in this way there is some hope of being delivered from arbitrariness.

3. ... *as Lord* ... The earliest creed of the Christian church was 'Jesus is Lord.' It is as Lord that the minister is to preach Christ Jesus. The pulpit is to be the throne of Jesus Christ, from which He may reign over a particular congregation by His word. Not the minister's platform, but the throne of Jesus Christ! It is the minister's task to strive to bring himself and his congregation back again and again under the discipline of the gospel, from which we are all of us ever prone to stray; for the Lord Jesus

Christ desires to make of minister and congregation His men and His women.

A true church is one which is open to the criticism, the control, and the guidance of the Lord and King of the church. And a true minister is one who so faithfully and humbly and perseveringly expounds the Scriptures that the Lord Jesus Christ is allowed to carry on with the congregation that conversation in which He wishes to engage them.

And here we have always to remember that the Bible has not been truly expounded until it has been allowed to strike home to the actual, concrete life of particular men and women. Far too many sermons remain in the air in vague generalities. But that is not how the Lord Jesus Christ wishes to speak to His people. Vague generalities, however pious and however eloquently expressed, do not make a Christian sermon. The passage of Scripture has to be applied; the preacher's work has not been properly done unless, overcoming the temptation to take refuge in vagueness and generalities, he allows it to indicate to his hearers quite explicitly and precisely how they, in the concrete particularity of their lives, are called to gratitude, to repentance, to renewal, to more faithful obedience. And it goes without saying, of course, that one cannot sincerely or effectively preach Christ as Lord from the pulpit unless one is honestly trying to obey Him as Lord in one's own life, day by day.

In a Reformed church the vows which the congregation make when a new minister is inducted mean that they as a congregation pledge themselves again to strive to let Christ be Lord over the life of the congregation and over their individual lives – not just in pious formulae but in reality.

4. *... and ourselves as your servants for Jesus' sake.*
This follows from what Paul has just said. When Jesus
Christ is truly acknowledged as Lord, this comes about.
The minister who sincerely preaches Christ as Lord
cannot but be the servant of his people. He will know that
he belongs to them (the Greek word used means 'slave'),
that it is his duty to labour for them, putting their true
interest before his own and not sparing himself.

But this does not mean that he is there to do their will,
to gratify their whims and fancies. The arbiter of what his
service of them is to be is not the congregation but Jesus
Christ alone. To be their servant for Jesus' sake cannot
mean to flatter and gratify their self-importance and self-
centredness, but only to seek their true Christian good.

These words of Paul's indicate the spirit of humility
which is a distinguishing mark of the true minister. They
forbid all lording it over the flock. They rule out of order
all thought of the ministry in terms of privilege and
prestige. The pastor must serve his people 'for Jesus'
sake', that is, on account of Jesus, who Himself 'came not
to be ministered unto, but to minister, and to give his life a
ransom for many'. When such humble, selfless service
becomes irksome, it is time to look again steadily at Jesus
Christ.

But there is a corollary to the minister's service of his
congregation: it is that minister and congregation
together are to be the servant of the community as a
whole, serving it both by the proclamation of the gospel
and by the humble, practical service of the sick and the
afflicted, the poor, the hungry, the underprivileged, and
the oppressed throughout the world. The congregation
which is not engaged in such service proclaims itself a
foreign body within the Church of Christ.

5. *Seeing it is God that said, Light shall shine out of darkness, who shined in our hearts to give the light of the knowledge of the glory of God in the face of Jesus Christ.* The effect of this verse is to turn our attention to the only source of strength by which minister and congregation can be faithful. It was not within the power of Paul to be true to his apostleship, nor is it within our power to be true to our calling. It is God's work in Christ for us and for all men and God's work by His Holy Spirit in us which are the basis and source of our obedience. We have to pray to God to continue and to perfect the good work which He has begun in us.

6. *But we have this treasure in earthen vessels, that the exceeding greatness of the power may be of God, and not from ourselves.* The covenant which is made between minister and congregation is always a covenant between sinners, between weak and frail and wayward and unworthy human beings. This truth may be for a little while partially veiled during the honeymoon period at the beginning of a new ministry; but the honeymoon never lasts a very long time. Then the truth has to be faced on either side, and it is of the greatest importance that each participant in the covenant should recognize himself as an earthen vessel and remember how much patience the other party needs must have.

In the light of this verse the minister will constantly remember that the real treasure of the gospel which his congregation professes and proclaims is contained in an earthen vessel. He will remember that his people are weak and frail; he will be understanding and sympathetic. He will not allow himself to be discouraged by the fresh evidences day by day provided for him that they are still sinners.

And similarly, the congregation which has called a brother-sinner to occupy – on its behalf and for its advantage – a peculiarly dangerous and exposed position will not forget, in the light of this verse, that its minister is very frail; they will bear with his weakness and honour the earthen vessel for the sake of the holy treasure it contains. If the gospel treasure is really there, the people will be grateful and will

> ... not grudge
> To pick out treasures from an earthen pot.

For it is God's will that His Word should come to us on frail human lips, that the exceeding greatness of the power may be of Him and not from ourselves.

6

TRUE RELIGION[1]

He hath shewed thee, O man, what is good; and what
doth the LORD require of thee, but to do justly, and
to love mercy, and to walk humbly with thy God?
(Micah 6.8.)

The passage we have just heard is one of the great biblical
definitions of true religion. Jesus perhaps had it in mind
when He summed up 'the weightier matters of the law' in
the words 'judgment, and mercy, and faith', which
amount to a paraphrase of this passage. It speaks to us
across the centuries with such directness that I need not
take time to go into the historical circumstances of its
composition.

The passage sets before us three requirements, three
essential elements of true religion. And the way in which
they are introduced indicates that the prophet did not
think of them as a burdensome imposition but as a
revelation of the divine will which is essentially gracious
and merciful.

I

The order in which they are mentioned is significant. The
prophet put 'to do justly' first, because, unlike a great
many of his contemporaries who imagined that God was

[1] Preached at the Durham University Degree Day Service in
Durham Cathedral on 26 June 1968.

126

satisfied with gifts and sacrifices, he knew that just conduct towards one's fellow-men is 'the real evidence of true religion', and that religious exercises without justice are an abomination to God. No one has a right to the name of a true Christian, unless he is seriously striving 'to do justly' in his dealings with his fellow-men.

But in indicating that the serious pursuit of justice is an indispensable mark of the Christian, I do not mean to suggest that those who stand in the biblical tradition have a monopoly of such concern. Those of us who were brought up on the Greek and Latin classics know well that there were men of noble integrity in the ancient pagan world. And there are, of course, many non-Christians today who are deeply and sincerely concerned to give to each man his due, to do what is equitable and fair. But in the Bible, in the light of the prophets and the law and of the teaching and example of Jesus and of His saving work, there is an understanding of justice deeper and broader than is to be found elsewhere, and having about it a generosity and warmth and humaneness which elsewhere the idea of justice often lacks. If the word 'just' strikes you as a rather cold word, suggesting a nicely calculated determination to do for one's fellows so much, but only so much, as they have an absolute right to expect, then it means that your idea of justice derives not from the Bible but from elsewhere. In the Bible the issues are sharpened and clarified. And it is where men's consciences have been instructed and made sensitive by a sincere and constant engagement with the Bible that the full meaning of justice in human relations is most clearly seen (though Christians and Christian bodies – to their shame be it said! – very often fall far short not only of the justice to which Holy Scripture points but also of the ordinary standards of decency accepted among pagans).

Notice that the prophet says, not 'admire justice' or 'engage in academic discussion of it', but 'do justly'. The Bible is interested in deeds. 'By their fruits ye shall know them', said Jesus, that is, by their deeds, not by their professions; for 'Not every one that saith unto me, Lord, Lord, shall enter into the kingdom of heaven; but he that doeth the will of my Father'. And this needs to be emphasized both against the dangerous half-truth one sometimes hears, that it's not what one does that matters but what one is (as though these could be separated), and also against the notion of some Christians that one can play off faith against deeds, which is a particularly disastrous distortion of evangelical truth (St Paul certainly opposed faith to a self-righteous confidence in one's works, to the illusion that one can put God in one's debt by them; but that is something entirely different from belittling the importance of deeds).

And the range of this requirement to do justly is as wide as the range of human relations. What is required is that we should strive in every human relationship to treat our fellow-man as, equally with ourselves, a man, a human being, to respect and defend his human dignity, in fact, to love our neighbour as ourselves – which is how Holy Scripture defines justice. It includes, for example, treating the other people in one's family not as amenities or mere extensions of one's own ego but as independent persons. It includes fair play in relation to one's employer or to those one employs, fair treatment of colleagues and rivals. It includes the conscientious fulfilment of one's responsibilities as a citizen, and, especially, in casting one's vote having regard not merely to one's own interest or that of a section of the community but to the good of all one's fellow-citizens and also the rights of one's fellow-men in other nations. It includes a resolute and unwearying resistance to the crying injustices in the world, and also the responsible and unselfish use of one's own money and resources. It includes, in academic work, such things as strict fairness to the views of others and arguing not for the sake of scoring a personal victory in debate but for the sake of the discovery and maintenance of the truth.

And it must be said that in Britain today, as in all other societies and in all past ages, to 'do justly' consistently requires courage, the courage to stand up and be counted, readiness to endure, if necessary, insults and misrepresentation and hatred, and to put one's career, one's prospects, one's happiness, at risk.

II

The second requirement is 'to love mercy'. There is, of course, a considerable overlap between this and the previous requirement. To some extent we have to do here with the same content viewed from a different angle. The Hebrew word, which 'mercy' here represents, is a particularly interesting word. It means 'kindness', 'mercy'; but in the Old Testament it is specially used where the parties concerned are thought of as being bound together by a definite bond. It carries the overtone of loyalty. Thus, when it is used with reference to God's mercy, it denotes His mercy to Israel after, rather than before, His establishment of His covenant with them. It is His steadfast loyalty to His covenant in spite of Israel's constant infidelity. It is also used to denote the loyal love to God which ought to be Israel's response to God's love. And, when it is used with reference to mercy shown by man to man, it denotes especially that kindness and loyal helpfulness which one Israelite owed to another as to a fellow-member of God's covenant people. That is no doubt what was primarily meant in this verse of Micah – though the address 'O man' suggests that the writer was himself aware of the relevance of his words beyond the confines of his own nation. But, as we seek to hear in this passage the word of God to ourselves, we have to see it in the light of the witness of the New Testament, and in that light we know that God has in Jesus Christ bound Himself not just to Israel or the Church but to the whole human race, to each and every man, and that there is therefore no human being who is not bound to us within the covenant of God's grace. What is required of us here then is steadfast loyalty to our fellow-men as those whom God loves, those for whom Christ died, and for whom He was raised up and exalted.

There is no lack of scope today – in all conscience – for such loyalty to our fellow-men. Many of you are no doubt as aware as I am of the human distress which on all sides cries out for human compassion and helpfulness, for that loyalty which does not desert a fellow-man in the time of his need, but stands by him to help and support him. There is distress enough in this country – one may think of the families without proper homes, the war-disabled, the unemployed, the immigrants who have been made to feel insecure and unwelcome, the patients in mental hospitals, the discharged prisoners struggling to re-establish themselves in society, the tramps, the dossers, the methylated spirit drinkers, to mention only some – while farther away there are the hungry millions who are victims of desperate, continuing poverty, the sufferers of brutal wars, and all the victims of oppressive and inhuman regimes. At the same time we see entrenched and embattled the forces of selfishness and heartlessness: the oppressors, the torturers, the exploiters, the ostensibly respectable who for the sake of trade, investments or political advantage provide support for oppression, the irresponsible ones who indulge in senseless luxury in the face of so much desperate need.

That loyalty to fellow-men is in short supply is only too clear. But our text reminds us that such loyalty is an indispensable element of true religion. To be a Christian involves refusing to abandon one's fellow-men in their wretchedness, and giving generously of one's strength and time and resources for their relief, refusing to regard any human life as cheap or expendable. ·

And the text speaks of *loving* mercy. That includes of course doing deeds of mercy, as we have seen; but it also means something more. We are to do all that steadfast loyalty demands, but we are to do it not just because we know we ought, but because we want, to do it. 'To love mercy' indicates an inner freedom, a commitment of the whole person, a total engagement of heart and mind and will. But this something more, this loving loyalty and compassion, is something we can hardly expect to see very often except where the third and last requirement of our text is being fulfilled.

III

The third requirement is 'to walk humbly with thy God'. The prophet left till last what he certainly regarded as basic to both the other requirements, that walking humbly with God – Jesus in the saying we referred to earlier called it faith – from which doing justly and loving mercy naturally flow. Most of us probably are willing to accept doing justly and loving mercy at least as ideals; but

I can imagine that some of you may feel that faith in God is another matter. It is in fact the crucial question – are you willing to walk humbly with God?

Walk humbly with *some* god you certainly will. We are just not free to choose whether we will have a god or not. 'There is no man who does not have his own god or gods as the object of his highest desire and trust, or as the basis of his deepest loyalty and commitment.'[1] The choice which is open to us is the choice between the true God, the living God to whom Holy Scripture bears witness, on the one hand, and, on the other hand, a variety of false gods.

It may be freely admitted that some of the false gods are less ignoble than others. For instance, a man may make the service of his fellows itself his god, the object of his highest desire, the basis of his deepest commitment, – or music, or art, or the advancement of knowledge in some particular field. Worship of such a god may indeed lead to a life which is not lacking in nobility and splendour. And yet even such gods are false gods which cannot save; for they are not the living God. But the most commonly worshipped false god is the false god whose name is Ego. And he is the ugliest and dreariest of them all, whose service, though it may look like freedom and independence and lordliness, is in reality nothing but shameful slavery. To walk humbly with the false god Ego is to become ever more and more sluttish in spirit. In his service you may become rich and influential and important; but, however rich and influential and important you become, you will, as a man or woman, get smaller and smaller.

When the prophet used the phrase 'thy God,' he

[1] K. Barth, *Evangelical Theology: an introduction*, translated by G. Foley, London, 1963, p. 3.

certainly did not mean any god his fellow-Israelite might choose for himself. He meant the one and only God who had an absolute right to his trust and allegiance, the right to be his God. By 'thy God' he meant moreover to suggest the goodness and graciousness with which God had stooped down to men in mercy and friendship, desiring not only to be the God of Israel as a whole, but to have fellowship with each individual Israelite and to be his God.

In the light of the New Testament witness to Jesus Christ, in the light of Gethsemane and Golgotha, we can see much more clearly what the words 'thy God' involve: how seriously and how patiently God has willed to be man's God, and at how great a cost He has given Himself to each one of us to be our God. This third requirement, then, is not simply a demand laid upon us; for it contains the gospel, the good news of the divine grace which is the presupposition of all the commandments of God. And in its light the first two requirements of our text are also no longer seen as a burden to weigh us down, but recognized as the summons to the freedom which God offers us in His Son.

For many of you today marks an important stage in your lives. Your university courses completed, you are about to set out on your careers. For others here tomorrow will bring the same sort of tasks as yesterday brought. But to all of us alike this word applies – this word in which God claims each one of us for Himself and for our fellow-men, and offers us life and joy: 'He hath shewed thee, O man, what is good; and what doth the LORD require of thee, but to do justly, and to love mercy, and to walk humbly with thy God?' May God give to each one of us to hear it and obey it!

7

COME UNTO ME[1]

Come unto me, all ye that labour and are heavy
laden, and I will give you rest. Take my yoke upon
you, and learn of me; for I am meek and lowly in
heart: and ye shall find rest unto your souls. For my
yoke is easy, and my burden is light.
(Matthew 11.28–30.)

The passage is familiar. Some of it we hear at the Lord's
Supper. For some of us, all of it will have unforgettable
associations with Handel's *Messiah*. It comes to us, as it
came to the first readers of the Gospel, with an authority
which the words will not have had for those who heard
them directly from the lips of Jesus Himself, namely, the
authority of His already accomplished death,
resurrection and ascension. The nature of the passage
makes it allowable, I think, for us to ask straight away
(without first attempting to discuss what may have been
the original historical context of the sayings it comprises),
What does the risen and exalted Lord have to say to us
now through it?

If the address, 'all ye that labour and are heavy laden'
should seem to any of us inappropriate to ourselves, we
had better take a good, long look at ourselves in the
mirror of the Bible. The stubborn, incontrovertible fact of
our moral weakness and deep selfishness will stare us in
the face, and we shall see ourselves unmasked as the

[1] Preached in King's College Chapel, Aberdeen, on 15 March 1981.

134

sinners that we are, labouring indeed and most miserably heavy laden. The picture which comes to my mind as I ponder my own condition and that of my fellow-men, as I can observe them, is of a poor little donkey, badly underfed, with painful sores, ridden by a great hulking bully who beats him without mercy and does everything which a rider ought never to do – except fall off. That cruel rider who has got himself astride each one of us is sin or – if we may use the word in the most serious sense it can bear – egotism.

And Jesus says to us, 'Come unto me'. Come to Me, labouring and heavy laden as you are, with all your troubles and sorrows and fears, with the knowledge – if you are honest with yourselves – that you have much, about which you ought to be ashamed, and weighed down – whether or not you have the theological sophistication and realism to recognize your condition – by the burden of that cruel and ugly bully that sits astride you, of whom you cannot rid yourselves, try how you may. Come to Me, commit yourselves to Me, just as you are.

What then? – 'and I will give you rest'. He offers us first the rest, the relief, of God's forgiveness. As the One, in whom the holy God Himself took on Himself the bitterness and shame of all men's sin, and bore it for them, so as to make available for them the costly pardon, which is altogether worthy of the holy and merciful God, because it does not in any way condone, or compromise with, our evil, or violate His truth and love; as the One, whom God raised from the dead and exalted, in whom our human nature has already been glorified, and who now intercedes for us as our High Priest; as this One, He offers us God's own forgiveness as firm, secure ground on which we can stand. And together with God's forgiveness He offers us a beginning of rest from our crazed self-centredness, a loosening of the hold of that cruel, demanding rider that is so good at not falling off, but good for nothing else, so that we may begin to have some freedom, some time and room and strength for God and for our fellow-men.

The rest Christ offers is certainly not idleness. The sequel speaks of a task. The rest is refreshment to fit us for His service. He begins the loosening of the load with which we have been laden; and at the same time He invites us to accept His yoke. 'Take my yoke upon you', He says. A yoke certainly means having a master and work to do. To have Jesus Christ as our Saviour is to have Him also as our Lord, to whom we owe obedience. He makes demands upon us. But how different are His demands from the demands of our egotism! Whereas the demands of our egotism are corrupt, degrading and absurd (for they are based on the lie that we are God), His demands are for purity of heart and life, for justice, mercy and truthfulness. He says to us: 'thou shalt love the Lord thy God with all thy heart, and with all thy soul, and with all thy mind, and with all thy strength' and 'thou shalt love thy neighbour as thyself', claiming us totally for God and our fellow-men. In His Discourse on the Final Judgment in Matthew 25, by revealing the mystery of His own personal presence in the poor and afflicted, He has made inescapably clear the obligation laid on all who would be His followers loyally to stand by their fellow-men who are wretched and distressed. For the man who wears Christ's yoke it cannot be a matter of indifference that the majority of his fellow-men are so constantly hungry that they could scarcely attend to Christ's invitation to the labouring and heavy laden, however powerfully it were preached to them. That wearing Christ's yoke involves support of such organizations as Christian Aid is fairly well grasped by many members of churches up and down the land. But the fact that wearing Christ's yoke has also a political dimension is, I suspect, much less adequately understood, and has to be affirmed with emphasis. In some kinds of state the scope of the Christian's political duty is rather narrowly limited (it was so in the Roman Empire in New Testament times); but for those Christians who are fortunate enough to be citizens of democratic states it includes using intelligently and unwearyingly all the constitutional means at their disposal – and they are more considerable than we are apt to think – to support just and compassionate policies and to oppose unjust, oppressive and heartless ones. It is, I think, actually harder to be a faithful Christian in a democracy than in an authoritarian state – not, of course, in the sense of being more dangerous or costly (for that it certainly is not!), but in the sense that one has so many more opportunities to act in defence of justice and human dignity, to miss which would be to neglect Christ Himself in the persons of His brethren.

The service indicated by 'Take my yoke upon you' includes, of course, service with the mind. An intelligent service is required of us. The further injunction, 'and learn of me', focuses attention on this duty of reflection and intellectual effort. It is not accidental that the word 'disciple' occurs so often in the Gospels and that Jesus is so often depicted as teaching and as being addressed as 'Teacher' or 'Rabbi'. To learn of Him is not only to try to follow the example of His life but also to allow one's mind to be instructed and illumined by His teaching. This should warn us against a certain anti-intellectual prejudice which flourishes from time to time in some Christian circles. If we are humble enough to learn of Him, we shall find ourselves driven toward more rigorous

137

and critical thinking in all areas of life and put on our guard against the proliferating lies and half-truths and shuffling ambiguities of the world around us. We shall regard with proper suspicion all mere assumptions which are treated as assured results and all over-confident experts who are unaware of the largeness of their ignorance and forgetful of the fact of their fallibility.

The following statement, 'for I am meek and lowly in heart', tells us one reason why He has the right to command us and to teach us, and at the same time indicates the nature of the example He has set us. In striking contrast with the powerful men and women of this world, who – some more, some less, but all to some extent – make use of their fellow-human-beings for their own self-aggrandisement, He is truly meek, gentle, humble of heart. He – the one Man who completely deserved the right to rule others because He never yielded to the temptation to abuse His power – 'came not to be ministered unto, but to minister, and to give his life a ransom for many', to be the Servant of all men and to pay with His own life for their release. And, though He is now exalted and glorified, He still waits to serve those whom He died and was raised to save. In Him we see what true authority is. It is He who is the standard by which every authority is measured and judged. Such is the pattern He has left for His people. One of the evening hymns in the *Church Hymnary* (642: a little gem, simple but profound) includes the lines:

> 'May we and all who bear Thy Name
> By gentle love Thy cross proclaim'.

They well sum up the life-style of the sincere Christian.

At first sight it may seem as if the sentence which

follows, 'and ye shall find rest unto your souls', is merely a repetition of the substance of the last part of verse 28 ('and I will give you rest'); but it is surely more natural, in view of the structure of these verses, to understand this promise somewhat differently. While in verse 28 the reference was to that rest which is the very basis of the Christian life, this last sentence of verse 29 is (in its context) surely a promise that in the actual serving of Christ and learning from Him we shall find rest to our souls. Throughout our lives the work of serving Him and submitting to His instruction, since He is who and what He is, will itself be for us continual refreshment of soul. And this promise leads naturally into the last verse of our text.

'For my yoke is easy, and my burden is light.' But how can this be true? Does not Jesus Himself bid those who would be His disciples take up their cross and warn them that they will be hated, reviled and persecuted for His sake? Is not Church history full of examples of sufferings undergone by Christians for their faith? Have not our own times seen many martyrs? And even in our own experience is it not sometimes hard and costly to be loyal to Christ? But the Bible bears witness to the other side of the picture also, to the delights of Christ's religion and to the truth that 'his commandments are not grievous' (1 John 5.3). In answer to the question, How can Christ's claim, 'My yoke is easy, and my burden is light', be true?, at any rate three things must be said.

The first is that He gives Himself for us and to us before ever He lays His yoke and burden on us, and He continues to give Himself to us all the time. This means that His commands are always set in the context of His giving Himself to us. It is characteristic of the Bible as a whole that in it always the divine grace is the presupposition of the requirements of God, that gospel is prior to law, God's self-giving to His commandments. So, for example, the first of the Ten Commandments is preceded by a statement setting forth God's mercy toward Israel ('I am the LORD thy God, which brought thee out of the land of Egypt, out of the house of bondage') and in Micah 6.8 ('He hath shewed thee, O man, what is good; and what doth the LORD require of thee, but to do justly, and to love mercy, and to walk humbly with thy God?') the basis of the three requirements is the truth (conveyed by the words, 'thy God') that the eternal God has willed to give Himself to men – at what cost to Himself the Cross declares – to be man's God, the God of each individual man.

The second thing is that Christ has already won the decisive battle of the war, so that the final issue is not in doubt. According to St John's gospel, Jesus, after warning His disciples frankly that in the world they must expect tribulation, went on to say, 'but be of good cheer: I have overcome the world'. That means that the yoke and the burden which He lays on us are the yoke and burden of obedience to Him, not of responsibility for the success of His cause. Of that responsibility we have no share – though Christian people often make the mistake of imagining that that responsibility rests on them. Thank God it does not! Our task is simply to be obedient to Him: the success of His cause is His concern, and that matter has already been decided.

The third thing is that God has given us His Holy Spirit to dwell in us; and an important part of the Spirit's work is to give us the freedom to begin to be obedient to Jesus Christ our Lord. He moulds us to the shape of Christ's yoke and so strengthens us that Christ's burden rests but lightly on us. The Christian finds that the yoke and burden of Christ are his delight. This is the fulfilment of God's promise (recorded by Jeremiah) to put His law in His people's inward parts and to write it in their hearts. And, as the Holy Spirit works His work in us, we shall be enabled to rebel more and more successfully against that hateful egotism that rides us. We shall receive increasing strength to give that unwanted rider a rougher and rougher ride. We may hope to throw him again and again into the mud and into the briers, and from time to time to add to his discomfiture a good bite and a sharp kick. He will always manage to scramble back upon us. We shall not be rid of him in this mortal life. But we may hope that he will become a more and more insecure rider, more and more uncomfortable on us, till finally, when we come to die in sure and certain hope of the resurrection to eternal life, he will die and be dead and done with for ever.

May each one of us discover in his or her own life the truth that Christ's service is perfect freedom and that, of all the privileges and joys and honours which can be had in this life, the greatest and richest and most precious beyond all compare is to wear the easy yoke of Jesus Christ and to carry His light burden all our days!

8

REMEMBER JESUS CHRIST[1]

Remember Jesus Christ, risen from the dead, of the seed of David, . . .

(2 Timothy 2.8.)

The Pastoral Epistles (1 and 2 Timothy and Titus) were addressed to pastors and are largely concerned with their duties. They combine counsel to them with instructions for the churches in their care. Our text stands out as summing up what these epistles have to say to pastors and their charges alike.

1. 'Remember Jesus Christ'

This may seem a rather strange thing to say. Was Timothy really in any danger of forgetting Jesus Christ? Do Christian ministers really need to be told to 'remember Jesus Christ'? Are they likely to forget Him? Is this exhortation – and the warning implicit in it – necessary for us who are here in this chapel this evening? Our presence here indicates that we are people who take our membership of Christ's Church seriously, and some of us are already ministers of the Word and Sacraments, while others are hoping to be ordained to that ministry. But we should be greatly mistaken, if we were to think that the injunction to 'remember Jesus Christ' was unnecessary for any of us. For the temptation to forget Christ is always with us, and will be till we die, whether in the form of frightening threat or – possibly more dangerously – under

[1] Preached in St John's College, Nottingham, on 7 May 1981.

142

an insidious variety of plausible disguises. If we recognize its existence, we may learn how great is our need of God's help: if we are unaware of it, then we are indeed in most dire peril.

We are constantly tempted to forget Christ by the pressure of the world's hostility to Him. In the ordination formula of the United Reformed Church, as of the former Presbyterian Church of England, there is a reference to 'trouble or persecution', which is a salutary reminder that the servant of Christ must be prepared for hostility. Archbishop William Temple once wrote: 'Not all that the world hates is good Christianity; but it does hate good Christianity and always will'. They are wise and true words. And I fear that there is a great deal of this good-Christianity-hating world comfortably ensconced within the Church itself! Against the temptation to forget Jesus Christ, to be ashamed of Him because (like Peter in the High Priest's courtyard) we are frightened, whether it comes to us from the world outside or from the entrenched worldliness inside the Church, may God give us the courage to remember and confess our Lord!

We are also constantly tempted to forget Christ by unconsciously usurping His place. Thus the preacher is tempted to preach himself instead of preaching Christ, to exploit the gospel itself as a means of showing off his own gifts and personality, using the pulpit as a stage for self-exhibition, forgetting that it is meant to be the throne of Jesus Christ. And how easy it is, quite unconsciously, to build a congregation around oneself instead of building them up on Christ, to win a personal following instead of helping people to follow Christ! It is sometimes so blatant that the outsider notices. More often it happens unobtrusively and decorously, though the result is equally disastrous. It is not at all surprising that congregations

143

tend to like to have it so; because the lordship of the minister or vicar is a lot less demanding than the Lordship of Jesus Christ. That it is also infinitely less rewarding does not appear at once.

And the fact that the name of Christ is much bandied about is no guarantee that He is really being remembered. Satan, as Paul testified, is well able to disguise himself as an angel of light (2 Corinthians 11.14); and aggressive and insatiable egotism is not seldom the dominant factor at work under the wraps of apparent evangelistic zeal, though unrecognized by those involved. The test, which our Lord's own teaching provides, as to the reality of our remembering Him is not how often we call Him 'Lord, Lord', but whether or not we do (or at least try to do!) the will of His Father (Matthew 7.21). And God's will includes not only trying to convert people, but doing justly and loving mercy (Micah 6.8). The temptation to forget Jesus Christ while busily talking about Him is one of which we who call ourselves 'evangelical' have special need to beware.

2. But the apostle does not leave matters at 'Remember Jesus Christ': he goes on to be more precise, adding two statements about Christ indicating how He is to be remembered. He does this because he realizes that it is easy to remember Him in ways which are tantamount to forgetting Him. You see there is a vast difference between, on the one hand, making much of our various private pictures of Christ, the ideas of Him which we have come to entertain, even what we may choose to call our experience of Him, and, on the other hand, remembering Christ as He is attested to us by Holy Scripture. The two phrases added serve to identify the true, the real Christ, as opposed to all our subjective imaginings of Him, which

can very easily be distorted and false. Let us now look briefly at these two phrases in turn, and then try to see what our text as a whole has to say to us.

(i)   *'risen from the dead'*
To remember Jesus Christ truly (in a Christian way) is to remember Him 'risen from the dead' – as the One who was crucified by sinful men like us, but has been raised up from the dead by His Father, and exalted. Paul defines what it is to be a Christian in Romans 10.9: 'if thou shalt confess with thy mouth Jesus as Lord, and shalt believe in thy heart that God hath raised him from the dead . . .'. It is the confession of the resurrection of Christ which is the true 'article by which the Church stands or falls' (*articulus stantis vel cadentis ecclesiae*): 'if Christ hath not been raised,' says St Paul (1 Corinthians 15.17), 'your faith is vain; ye are yet in your sins'. It is the Resurrection which attests Jesus of Nazareth as God's Son; His earthly life, His ministry and passion, as God's saving deed, the world's redemption. That He is risen is the astounding and all-important news, to be ignorant of which is to be altogether out of date, to be living not in today, nor in a fairly modern past, but in a centuries-outmoded past. This is the truth which some of our clergy will have to learn, if they are ever to catch up with the times!

(ii)   *'of the seed of David . . .'*
The words tell us of His historical life in its historical setting as the legal Son of Joseph and thereby of the family of David. They tell us of His Jewishness, of His being the Messiah of Israel, the fulfilment of the hopes of the men of the Old Testament, and – what is more important – His being the fulfilment of God's promises in the Old

145

Testament. They indicate to us that the Old Testament is indispensable, if we are to know Jesus Christ as He is.

3. *Application of this text as a whole to us*
The two explanatory phrases may be said to sum up the Bible's witness to Jesus Christ. We may compare Romans 1.3–4 where the same two facts of the Resurrection and of Christ's being of the seed of David are underlined. So what the text as a whole says to us is: Remember Jesus Christ, as He is attested by the Scriptures (by the united witness of the Old Testament and the New), remember Him in the fullness of the biblical witness to Him.

As a good many of you are expecting to be ordained, I am going to take the liberty of speaking for the next minute or two particularly to those of you who are in that position. You will be called on to preach sermons. One duty of a minister in the Church of England as in other churches is to be 'a faithful Dispenser of the Word of God' (as the Book of Common Prayer has it). I beseech you in God's Name, when you have to prepare sermons, remember Jesus Christ – remember Him as He is attested to us in the Bible. It is important, of course, that you should have a real, deep, personal experience of Christ. But God in His pity save your congregations from having to endure the proclamation of their pastors' experience! Your experience is not to be the content of your preaching (though from time to time it may well be a more or less useful confirmation of your message). Your experience of Christ will anyway be very limited and poor by comparison with the reality of Christ. The content of your preaching is rather to be Jesus Christ as witnessed to by Holy Scripture – Christ in the fullness of the Bible's testimony to Him. The Barmen Confession of 1934 contains the words 'Jesus Christ, as He is attested to us in

Holy Scripture, is the one Word of God, which we have to hear and which we have to trust and obey in life and in death'. Have no fear that such a concentration is going to result in a confining, narrowing, impoverishing of your message. Quite the contrary is true. It is those who have self-centredly and idolatrously insisted on proclaiming their own personal experience as the chief burden of their sermons and those who in a variety of other ways have managed to forget Jesus Christ as attested by Scripture, who have reduced preaching in so many churches in Britain (and elsewhere too, of course) to something unutterably boring. God calls you to preach Christ in the fullness of the Bible's witness to Him, and so as the only but also the altogether sufficient Saviour and Lord, not only of the Church, but of all men, and indeed of God's whole creation. So to preach Him (striving always to remember Him as He really is) will be immeasurably to extend and enlarge your own and your people's horizons, understanding, sympathies. As attested in the Scriptures, Christ is God's gift of His own Self in grace and mercy to all men and for all men, the true hope of all mankind and all creation; He is also the One in whom God has claimed each one of us and all men for Himself and for the neighbour. So in the fullness of the Bible's witness to Him He is relevant to every part of the world's life, God's illuminating, judging, healing, liberating, saving Word.

If you do thus 'remember Jesus Christ, risen from the dead, of the seed of David' in your preaching, you will be enabled to proclaim the gospel confidently and joyfully as the true gospel which it is. The gospel of Christ certainly deserves to be preached confidently and joyfully always – and never, never dolefully, tediously, apologetically, doubtingly, as it is (I fear) far too often preached.

Truly to remember Christ in your preaching will

147

involve serious, strenuous, persistent study of your Bible. In God's Name I beg you never to allow yourselves to be persuaded that you are too busy for such study, for if you do, you will be betraying those entrusted to your care. But to remember Christ will also involve a diligent application to the issues of the present day, to the newspaper as well as to the Bible, and of course to understanding your people. The Word of God has not been properly preached until the text has been brought to bear concretely and particularly on your own life and the lives of your congregations. The Westminster *Directory for the Publick Worship of God* wisely says that the preacher 'is not to rest in general doctrine, although never so much cleared and confirmed, but to bring it home to special use, by application to his hearers: which albeit it prove a work of great difficulty to himself, requiring much prudence, zeal, and meditation, and to the natural and corrupt man will be very unpleasant; yet he is to endeavour to perform it in such a manner, that his auditors may feel the word of God to be quick and powerful, and a discerner of the thoughts and intents of the heart'.

I have spoken about your preaching. I know full well, of course, that your preaching will only be one part of what you are called to do. But to concentrate on this one part was not, I think, a mistake; for you will find that, if your preaching is *really* faithful, then the rest will follow naturally. If you 'remember Jesus Christ' in the sense of our text in your preparation and preaching of sermons, then you will know that your visiting of the homes of your people and your fulfilment of your part in the life of the wider community and also your own personal life must be continuous with your preaching, an extension of it, and of one piece with it. Anything else would be intolerable. So may God use you to bring to the weak, selfish, anxious, struggling lives of the people of the parishes, which you are called to serve, the judging, healing, strengthening, saving message of God's grace in Jesus Christ!

I have spoken for too long to one group of you. Let me say to those of you who will remain lay men and women that for you too remembering Jesus Christ has to do with every part of your lives. And in some ways, at any rate, it is harder for you than for the ordained. I think it is still true (even in this very pagan period of our country's history) that the ordinary pagan expects a Christian minister to stand for Jesus Christ and, in his heart of hearts (whatever he may say), despises him utterly, if he is not ready clearly and firmly to confess his Lord. That is a very great help to him, if he has any sense. But for you it is different. You have not this protection, which a clergyman has; and the pressures of the world are exceedingly strong. All the same, God calls you too to remember Jesus Christ, whatever trouble or persecution may arise. And He can give you the necessary courage.

Let me say one final thing which concerns every one of us. We all have those who under one form or another bear a pastoral responsibility toward us. They have a right to our prayers. Let us also expect the right things from them. This will be a marvellous support for them. Let us expect them faithfully to bring to bear on our lives (in their conduct of worship, their preaching, their visitations, their administering and organizing) the message of God's grace in Jesus Christ. They may be able to give us various other things which we may gratefully receive; but this is the one thing which really matters, the one thing we have a right and duty to look for from them. This will not be comfortable for us in the sense of being comfortable for our self-complacence and selfishness: it is sometimes profoundly uncomfortable to have a faithful pastor. But the uncomfortable, disturbing, humbling, yet healing and liberating, comfort of God's grace in Jesus Christ is the only true comfort to be had in this mortal life, and, if we are wise, we shall desire it with all our heart!

Every one of us here is very weak and altogether unworthy of Jesus Christ. But may we be humble enough to trust our weak and wayward lives to Him and to let Him make something worth while out of them, to His glory!

9

JOY, PEACE, HOPE[1]

Now the God of hope fill you with all joy and peace
in believing, that ye may abound in hope, through
the power of the Holy Ghost.

(Romans 15.13.)

Paul, who was in or near Corinth at the time, wanted to
inform the Christians in Rome of his plan to visit them,
after first making a necessary visit to Jerusalem. Since the
great majority of them had never seen him, he felt the need
to introduce himself to them. For him the most important
thing about an apostle was the message he had been
commissioned to proclaim. So it is hardly surprising that
he should decide that the best way to introduce himself
would be to incorporate in his letter an account of the
gospel, the good news, of Jesus Christ as he had come to
understand it. Several practical considerations such as the
strategic position of the Christians in the imperial capital,
the likelihood that a letter sent to them would also be read
by Christians from other places, and, perhaps also, the
prospect of a few weeks of relative freedom from pressure,
may have encouraged him to make this account specially
full and careful. At any rate, of the sixteen chapters of
Romans some fourteen (1.16b–15.13) are a magnificently
constructed piece of theological writing which has
gripped and fascinated thoughtful Christians for more
than nineteen centuries and defeated all attempts of
commentators to do it justice.

[1] Preached in St Salvator's Chapel, St Andrews, on 27 February
1983.

151

Our text marks the end of this great theological statement. It indicates what Paul wants – and confidently expects – God to do to the Christians in Rome: 'May the God of hope fill you with all joy and peace in believing, so that you may abound in hope by the power of the Holy Spirit'. But why did Paul think that to express this wish was a particularly appropriate way to conclude his account of the gospel? Why did he single out these three things – joy, peace, hope? And why did he put special emphasis on the third both by describing God as 'the God of hope' (that is, 'the God who is the source of hope') and by the structure of his sentence (they are to be filled with joy and peace, in order that they may abound in hope)?

A good reason for mentioning *joy* and placing it first is not far to seek; for joy is the natural consequence of good news, and Paul has been expounding the good news about Jesus Christ. At the very beginning of his letter he has described himself as an apostle by God's calling, set apart for the work of proclaiming God's message of good news. In 1.16 he has declared that he is not ashamed of the good news, and gone on to define it as God's saving power, and to claim that in its on-going proclamation God's gift of righteousness is being revealed and offered to men. If the Roman Christians have attended to the fourteen chapters which precede our text, they will have learned much about the good news of Christ. The joy to which Paul refers is the special joy which the good news of Christ, preached and believed, creates. Paul wants God to fill them with all joy in believing, that is, so to confirm their faith in Jesus Christ that their joy which is its natural effect may continually be increased and deepened, and may more and more fill their hearts and transform their lives. And what Paul wants and expects for the Roman Christians we may hear as God's promise for us.

Since a Christian is some one who has heard and believed God's message of good news, a joyless Christian is a contradiction in terms. Great joy is a mark of the Christian life. But it needs to be said that it would be arrogant in any of us to assume that our particular way of showing our joy in the Lord is the only proper way: we ought to allow for differences of temperament and other differences between Christians. It must also be made clear that, along with joy, we must expect both a share of the sorrows and afflictions which are common to all men and also a share of those which come to Christians because they are Christians. Paul has already in Romans spoken more than once of persecution. He is well aware that the world which has rejected and crucified Jesus Christ will also hate and persecute all who are faithful to Him. We should be deceiving ourselves if we emphasized the reality and the wonder of Christian joy in such a way as to obscure the fact that it is experienced in the midst of dangers and afflictions. The eloquent last paragraph of Romans 8 shows Paul's realistic view of the life of the Church under the cross. But Paul expects his fellow-Christians in Rome – and we should remember that a large proportion of them will have been slaves, their persons terribly exposed to the arbitrary power of masters and mistresses – to be filled with joy, a joy which can co-exist with grief and suffering, disappointment, frustration, persecution, captivity and the threat of death. There is nothing superficial about the joy to which Paul refers. It is strong, deep, enduring, because it has its origin in God, in what He has done for us in Christ, and in the work of His Spirit in us.

In the second place, Paul wants God to fill the Roman Christians with *peace*. The word 'peace' is used by Paul in various senses. So in Romans 5 it denotes the state of peace with God which God has brought about by His work of reconciliation, while elsewhere it refers to peace between men. Again, it can be used in a comprehensive sense as more or less equivalent to 'salvation'. But it is also used to denote something inward, an interior peace, which does indeed spring from peace with God but is not identical with it. The word is so used here, where Paul speaks of God's filling the persons whom he is addressing with peace. He wants God to fill the Christians in Rome 'with all . . . peace in believing', that is, with the fullness of that inner peace which results from faith in Christ. There are numerous other sorts of inward peace which Paul certainly does not mean, like the peace of self-complacency, the peace of an insensitive conscience, the peace of slothfulness, the peace of an illusory sense of security, or the peace which is only an inner cosiness where all outward circumstances are comfortable. He does not even mean the peace of an unquestioning faith. God does not desire a 'love which asks no questions' even to Himself. Plenty of questions are asked in the Epistle to the Romans. Baffling problems are honestly raised.

The interior peace which Paul desires for the Roman Christians is that which he calls elsewhere 'the peace of God', that is, the authentic inward peace which God, and only God, can give, that inward peace which, as he tells the church in Philippi, is able to mount guard over believers' hearts and thoughts, keeping their minds and thoughts, their emotions and desires, under the discipline and protection of Jesus Christ. Paul knows that, from without, the world's hostility will continually batter and its allurements continually entice, while, from within, there will continually rise up doubts and fears and all the powers of indwelling sin. He knows that in the believer, in whom the Holy Spirit is at work and to whom God's grace and God's law have been made clearly known, a far fiercer and more serious conflict is to be expected than is possible in the unbeliever. Paul's prayerful wish for the Christians in Rome is also God's word of promise for us, that, in the midst of all the strife and tumult both within us and without, His guardian peace shall possess our inner man, that self which is being re-created by God's Spirit, holding it firmly bound to Jesus Christ our Lord with bonds which cannot be broken, and enabling us to serve God with a quiet heart, getting on effectively and without fuss with the work of obeying Jesus Christ, undistracted by the disabling restlessness to which our nature is so prone. Certain it is that without the presence of this guardian peace there can be little progress in the Christian life.

In the third place Paul speaks of *hope*. Paul wants God to fill the Roman Christians with all joy and peace, in order that they may abound in hope. On this third thing special emphasis is placed. The sentence treats the Roman Christians' being filled with joy and peace as means to the end of their abounding in hope. It hardly needs to be said that, as there are other sorts of joy and other sorts of inward peace besides the joy and peace to which Paul refers, so too there are many other hopes cherished by men besides that of which he speaks. But, soon or late, they prove illusory. To use the expression which he took from the Old Testament – they 'put to shame'. The hope he refers to is that which comes from God, that which is God's gift. Hence the description of God as 'the God of hope' at the beginning, and the inclusion of the phrase 'by the power of the Holy Spirit' at the end, of the verse. God gives this hope through the indwelling of His Spirit.

That Paul should give special emphasis to hope here is not surprising in view of the place which hope has in what precedes this verse. Paul has spoken of Abraham's believing God's promise in hope against all hope, that is, hoping steadfastly when everything in his circumstances and condition seemed to mock his hope; of the Christian's exulting in hope of the glory of God, that is, in hope of sharing in the final accomplishment of God's good and glorious purpose for His creation; of hope's being strengthened and confirmed by being tested by troubles; of the indwelling of the Spirit as the guarantee of eternal life; of our being heirs of God, joint-heirs with Christ; of the earnest expectation of the whole sub-human creation; and of the approach of God's day which already – for those who have eyes to see – begins to light up the darkness of this present age. It is not surprising that in 15.4 it is our being enabled to hold fast our hope which is singled out as the special benefit of the comfort of the Scriptures; for to hold on to our hope is to abide in Christian faith, while to abandon it is to cease to be Christian.

In view of what has gone before in Romans there is nothing surprising in Paul's emphasis on hope in our text. But has abounding in hope anything to do with us who live in a day of widespread and thoroughly understandable hopelessness? Reasons for hopelessness are obvious enough. In our own country we see massive, and still mounting, unemployment with all the misery which it means not just for the unemployed themselves but also for their families. And surely more utterly depressing than even that appalling mass of human frustration and misery itself is – for any who are reflective and morally sensitive – the shameful equanimity with which so many of us who are not directly affected by unemployment are able to contemplate the plight of those who are. We see the chasm between rich and poor in our country being constantly widened and deepened, and the weak and disadvantaged being compelled to bear a disproportionately large, and continually increasing, share of the nation's burden, while a very considerable measure of relief is given to the richest. We see education suffering grievous damage, the serious effects of which will still be working themselves out, to the detriment of our national life, long after the financial resources which have been taken away have been restored. It would seem that our nation as a whole has lost its way and got its priorities disastrously wrong. And, when, beyond the domestic bleakness of Britain, we see oppression, torture and lies arrogantly triumphing in so many lands, and half the world's population suffering hunger which ends only with death while others obscenely squander vast sums of money on heartlessly ostentatious luxury, and, above all, the menace of the nuclear arms race, we can hardly wonder that many have embraced despair.

With so little evidence of humanity or of wisdom, of breadth of vision, sympathy or knowledge, among those who wield great political and military power, and with so much to suggest that momentous decisions may be made on the basis of obsessions and of simplistic slogans unreflectingly repeated rather than on the basis of adequate knowledge and intelligent thought and a real concern about right and wrong, there is, indeed, humanly speaking, small reason to be hopeful.

In this world of 1983 with all its hopelessness, the Word of God speaks to us of abounding in hope. It is important to recognize that this hope is, indeed, primarily hope for what is beyond this present life and beyond history as we know it: hope of life with Christ after death; hope of Christ's coming in glory as Judge and Redeemer; hope of God's triumphant accomplishment of His good and gracious purpose for us and for all men and for His whole creation, His bringing all things to a goal worthy of Himself as the almighty and faithful Creator. But, far from being an opiate to lull us into a supine acceptance of the injustices of the present, this hope (provided it is the genuine thing) will compel us to challenge, courageously and resolutely, evil and folly, wherever they present themselves.

If we have properly heard our text and understood it in the light of what precedes it in the Epistle to the Romans, then we can, and must, declare with confidence that, even should the wickedness and incredible stupidity of the world's rulers and those who follow them bring upon us untold misery and on this earth a more terrible, and far longer, dark age than any it has as yet suffered (which God in His pity forfend!), our hope shall still not fail of fulfilment. The God who has revealed Himself in Jesus Christ will still be in command, in everlasting majesty and mercy. It always will be, as it is, and always has been, He, and He alone, who reigns. Those who have the hope of which Paul speaks will strive with determination both to turn men away from the madness of the nuclear arms race, and also to get on boldly and competently and energetically with all those other works of justice and mercy for which those who are sons and daughters of God have been set free. How badly the world needs today Christians who abound in hope! May Paul's wish for the Roman Christians of the 50s be fulfilled also for us! May the God of hope fill us too with all joy and peace in believing, so that we may abound in hope by the power of the Holy Spirit, to His glory and to our neighbours' good!

10

THE RESURRECTION APPEARANCE TO MARY MAGDALENE[1]

When she had thus said, she turned herself back, and beholdeth Jesus standing, and knew not that it was Jesus. Jesus saith unto her, Woman, why weepest thou? whom seekest thou? She, supposing him to be the gardener, saith unto him, Sir, if thou hast borne him hence, tell me where thou hast laid him, and I will take him away. Jesus saith unto her, Mary. She turneth herself, and saith unto him in Hebrew, Rabboni; which is to say, Master. Jesus saith to her, Touch me not; for I am not yet ascended unto the Father: but go unto my brethren, and say to them, I ascend unto my Father and your Father, and my God and your God. Mary Magdalene cometh and telleth the disciples, I have seen the Lord; and *how that* he had said these things unto her.

(John 20.14–18.)

Mary Magdalene had been to the tomb before daybreak. Finding that the stone had been rolled back from the entrance of the tomb and that the body of Jesus had disappeared, she had run back for help. Then, when Peter and the other disciple had run to the tomb, she had followed them. When they had gone away, she had lingered on alone. As she wept, she had stooped to look into the tomb, and had seen two angels sitting where the

[1] Sermon preached in Waddington Street United Reformed Church, Durham, on 22 April 1984.

159

body of Jesus had lain, one at the head and one at the feet. They had said to her, 'Woman, why weepest thou?' Mary was too absorbed in her grief to recognize the angels, and her brief conversation with them was interrupted by the approach of a stranger, whom she turned to see, but did not recognize. She was probably too absorbed in her grief to see clearly, and the thought of seeing Jesus again alive had never entered her head. Moreover, the risen body of Jesus, though identical with the body which had been crucified and which had lain in the tomb, had been mysteriously transformed – 'changed', as Paul puts it – into resurrection body, glorified body, so that it was now no longer subject to the limitations of His earthly life and could appear or vanish as He willed, and be more, or less, easily recognizable according to His will.

Jesus repeated the angels' question with the significant addition of 'whom seekest thou?', delicately referring to the fact that her distress had to do with the loss of a dear one. Thinking that He was the gardener, she supposed that He might have had a hand in removing the body, and her thoughts were so completely taken up with her Lord that she assumed that the gardener must know to whom she referred: 'Sir, if thou hast borne him hence . . .'. If the gardener will but show her where he has laid Him, she herself will take Him away. But, having made her request, she at once turned away, as if she had already given up any hope that he might be able to help her. Then suddenly with a single word He made Himself known to her – 'Mary!' And she at once turned back to Him, and with one word answered Him – 'Rabboni!', 'My Master!', which summed up everything, her recognition, her faith, her love. She apparently at the same time threw herself at His feet, and clasped them. But Jesus bade her let go. She had held Him long enough to be reassured. Now she had to learn that she had not received Him back like another Lazarus, merely restored to a further period of quite ordinary natural life, to a life which must once more succumb to death. Jesus's resurrection was something very different from that of Lazarus. Unlike him, Jesus had been given complete and final deliverance from death. Christ, having once been raised from the dead, dieth no more. Mary had to learn that her Master was to ascend to His Father, and that she had willingly to let Him go, in order that she might henceforth have Him for ever, everywhere. And now she had to take the good news to the disciples. It was for them too, and, through them, for all mankind.

Such is the narrative of these verses. Let us now for a few minutes look back at some of its features to see what they have to say to us as we celebrate together Christ's Holy Supper this Easter Sunday morning.

The first human being to see the risen Lord is a woman. The prominence of women in the Easter narratives in the Gospels is important for two different reasons. (i) It is a very strong confirmation of the truth of the Resurrection, since it is something which the early Church would certainly never have invented. Among the Jews of the first century a woman's testimony was legally acceptable only in certain exceptional matters – for example, a widow's witness as to the death of her husband was accepted. But generally women were not recognized as credible witnesses. That is why St Paul in 1 Corinthians 15 lists only male witnesses to the Resurrection: he was giving a list of legally acceptable witnesses. His omission of the women had nothing to do with any contempt for women on *his* part: his letters provide clear evidence that he was far from being 'anti-women' himself (despite common ideas to the contrary). The prominence of women in the

Gospel Empty Tomb and Resurrection Appearance narratives is only explicable as historical fact.

(ii) The other reason why it is important is of course that it sets God's authority decisively once for all against every notion that women are spiritually inferior to men. The Church has indeed been – and still often is – recalcitrant and stubborn in its reluctance to accept this; but the fact that the first human eyes to see the risen Lord, and the first human voice to bear the message, were female has given the lie to all arrogant male claims of superiority, once for all.

There seems to be no good reason for identifying Mary of Magdala with the woman of loose morals in Luke 7.36ff (though this identification has been widely accepted in the western Church), but she was apparently someone who had been seriously ill mentally or physically (Luke 8.2) and whom Jesus had healed. In choosing to show Himself first to her the risen Christ made manifest what a German New Testament scholar (E. Stauffer) calls His 'royal chivalry'. He makes it His first task to help and comfort her. He realizes her need of His support – her special need – and deals with it with amazing tenderness and sensitivity.

Jesus makes Himself known to Mary Magdalene by addressing her by name – 'Mary!' Much earlier in St John's Gospel (in chapter 10) it is written of the Good Shepherd: 'he calleth his own sheep by name, and leadeth them out' and, again, 'the sheep follow him: for they know his voice'. My brothers and sisters, this Easter morning the Good Shepherd, our risen Lord Jesus Christ, calls each one of us by name. It may possibly be that even in this gathered company of worshippers we are not all of us known to each other by name, but He certainly knows each one of us as an individual, in all the circumstances of our individual lives. In a day of terrible divisions and isolation and loneliness in this and other lands, He calls each person by his or her name. And His call is addressed not just to the individuals who gather for worship. He died for *all*, and He wants to claim each single one of the sons and daughters of men – even the most disobedient and rebellious, the most truculently sinful and wandering. Those whom the Father has given Him hear His voice and know Him; but we must never, never assume that because God has not yet given someone to His Son, therefore He never will. We must not accept the present fact of a man's or a woman's unbelief as an unalterable fact. No human being can present Almighty God with an 'eternal fact'!

So let us hear in Jesus' addressing Mary by her name His gracious call to each one of us and at the same time His mercy and grace for all the individuals which make up the population of this planet, most of them in apparently hopeless need and deprivation and misery, and many of them in hideous hardness of heart and callous selfishness, contemptuous of their fellow-human beings – and of the eternal God.

Mary at once recognized the One who called her by her name. She answered with the one word 'Rabboni!' – 'My Master!', which expressed altogether her recognition, her faith, her love. Let us pray to God to enable us, like Mary, to recognize our Lord Jesus Christ, as He speaks to us this day in His graciousness and mercy, and to give Him again our trust and our love, as our Master and Teacher, our Lord and our God.

On the first Easter morning Mary was allowed not only to hear with her outward ears her Saviour's voice and actually with her eyes to see Him, but also for a few moments to cling to His feet to be reassured and strengthened. But then came the command to let go, because He would ascend to His Father and she and the others who believed in Him had to learn to walk by faith and not by sight. In the long centuries of the Church's history Christians have had to be content with the testimony of those who at the first did actually hear and see and touch, and all their lives to walk by faith, not by sight. We belong to those following generations. And for us there is the special blessing pronounced by Jesus (spoken to Thomas): 'blessed are they that have not seen, and yet have believed'.

But Mary is not only told to let go of Jesus's feet: she is given a commission, 'go unto my brethren, and say to them, I ascend unto my Father and your Father, and my God and your God'. Luther in one of his Easter sermons observed that the whole of the gospel may be said to be summed up in that 'my brethren'. The Son of God calls *us* His brothers and sisters. What a tremendous thing it would be, Luther observed, if only the king of France or the king of England were to say to one of us ordinary people, 'You shall be my brother'; how much more wonderful that the King of kings Himself calls us His brothers![1]

Our text ends with a very quiet, sober, matter of fact sentence: 'Mary Magdalene cometh and telleth the disciples, I have seen the Lord, and how that he had spoken these things unto her'. Mary obeyed Jesus, and became the first herald of the Resurrection, the witness of the risen Lord to the apostles. The apostles themselves were not given the privilege to be the first to bear the message that Jesus is risen, and we certainly cannot be the first. But we, like the apostles, can follow – and surely

[1] *Martin Luthers Evangelien-Auslegung* 5, ed. E. Mülhaupt, Göttingen, 1950, pp. 369–372.

must follow – Mary's example and be witnesses all the rest of our lives, by word and deed, to the good news that Jesus our Lord is risen. What the risen Lord assures us individually, calling each one of us by name as He called Mary by her name, we cannot possibly keep to ourselves; for it concerns all men and women and children everywhere – and the whole of God's creation.

11

CHARGE TO MINISTER AND CONGREGATION[1]

And I, brethren, when I came unto you, came not with excellency of speech or of wisdom, proclaiming to you the mystery of God. For I determined not to know anything among you, save Jesus Christ, and him crucified. And I was with you in weakness, and in fear, and in much trembling. And my speech and my preaching were not in persuasive words of wisdom, but in demonstration of the Spirit and of power: that your faith should not stand in the wisdom of men, but in the power of God.

(1 Corinthians 2.1–5.)

Since in these verses St Paul is speaking to the Corinthian Christians about his own ministry among them, we may with good reason expect God to have something to say through them both to you, David, as you enter on your new ministry and also to those of us who have just accepted you as our pastor. I am not going to try to draw out from this passage two quite distinct charges (one to the minister and one to the congregation); for Paul is actually addressing the church as he speaks of his own ministry, and, if those of us who belong to this congregation listen attentively enough to what is here said about Paul's, and David's, ministry, we shall find it

[1] Sermon preached at the induction of the Rev David Holt Roberts in Waddington Street United Reformed Church, Durham, on 23 June 1984.

includes a charge to ourselves. We shall receive a deeper insight into what our minister is called by God to try to do, and therefore a deeper insight into what we ought to look for from him, and into how we can help him, and how, working together with him, we can be a better Christian congregation.

I. We may take verses 1 and 2 together. In verse 1 Paul states that, when he had come to Corinth proclaiming the gospel, he had not relied on excellence of speech or wisdom. We need to be careful how we understand this. Paul hardly means that in his preaching he had paid no attention at all to excellence of speech or wisdom. That he could be, and sometimes was, very eloquent indeed, is clear enough from his letters to any one who is competent to judge Greek style. What he means is that he had not relied on eloquence, cleverness, wisdom. And the reason for this he indicates in verse 2. It was because of his concern with something of immeasurably greater importance.

And, when in verse 2 he says that he had resolved to know nothing, in his dealings with the Corinthians save Jesus Christ, he clearly does not mean that he had resolved to know nothing at all other than Christ. Clearly Paul knew, and would continue to know, many other things. For example, he knew at least three languages, probably four. He knew a good deal of Rabbinic biblical exegesis. His knowledge of the culture of the Greek-speaking Gentile world cannot have been negligible. He had a working knowledge of the administration of the Roman empire. He was not at a loss in dealing with Jewish or Roman authorities. He had the practical knowledge necessary for getting about the world. He must have had a quite considerable geographical

167

knowledge. He certainly does not mean that he had determined to jettison all this knowledge. What he means is that he had decided that he would let Christ alone be the standard by which he would measure all things, the key to understanding, the controlling factor of all his thinking and doing, the content of his preaching.

You, David, have come to us with many gifts, gifts which this congregation has noted and appreciated – your powers of leadership, your learning, your ability to express your message interestingly and memorably, your cheerful, attractive personality, your ready smile, your ability to get alongside young and old alike. These things – and more besides – are God's gifts to you, and, through you, to us and to Durham. Use them to God's glory. But do not rely on them. Rely only on Jesus Christ. Proclaim only Him.

Paul did not end his sentence with 'save Jesus Christ', but added the words 'and him crucified'. He certainly did not mean by this that he would preach nothing about Christ except His cross. For Paul, as for the early Church generally, the focus-point of faith was the present work of the exalted Christ (hence the earliest creed, 'Jesus is Lord'). But the exalted Lord was the One who had been crucified. True, if the Cross had been the end of the story, there would have been no good news. But, equally, there would have been no good news for sinful men, had not God Himself borne in the person of His own dear Son the sin of the world once for all upon the cross. Paul was aware of the Corinthians' inclination to think too little of the Cross. They were inclined to be too keen on triumph and glory. Paul had to chide them (in chapter 4) for imagining they were already 'reigning' – already glorified and triumphant. They liked to dwell on Christ's glory and on their sharing it, and were disinclined to remember always the weakness, disgrace and agony which had been the price of their redemption.

You, David, are indeed to preach Jesus Christ as Lord, Lord of His church and also Lord of the world, of history, of the universe. But never allow us to forget that the One who is Lord of all is the same One that was crucified. Remind us constantly of His cross as the revelation both of the meaning of man's sinfulness and also of the greatness of God's love. Remind us too of the fact that the cross is the sign of the true church's life on earth, of the fact that the true church is throughout history the church under the cross, whose life is marked by suffering, self-sacrifice, compassion, service, truthfulness, integrity – in fact, by those very things which are the direct opposite to all that this age which is passing away stands for, with its empty pomp, its cult of power, of 'go-getting', of ruthless competitiveness, of exploitation of all that can be exploited, its violence and terror and lies.

II.   In the second place, Paul goes on in verse 3 to tell the Corinthian church that he was with them 'in weakness'. They were not impressed by weakness. They prided themselves on their strength as Christians, on the victory aspect of the Christian life. Paul was conscious of his own weakness – and aware of theirs.

You too, David, are weak. You will fulfil your ministry among us in weakness. And we, who are to be your care, are all of us weak and frail. Make no mistake about it. In our different circumstances and different ways we all of us fail again and again to do the good that we would, and do again and again the evil which we would not. Some of us may sometimes be tempted to forget our frailty. There is always in the church a dangerous proneness to triumphalism of one sort or of another. God grant,

David, that you may always remember your own weakness and that you may see to it that we are not allowed to forget ours! What has just been said should certainly not discourage either you or us. True courage eschews illusions. And no persons are weaker than those who imagine themselves strong. But God's strength is made perfect in our human weakness. God is able to do great things through you, David, and through this congregation, and I for one have great hope and confidence that He will do them. I want to say this emphatically.

Paul goes on to say that he was with the Corinthians 'in fear, and in much trembling'. He is certainly not referring to fear of the Corinthian Christians. He was not afraid of them. And you, David, must certainly not fear us – nor any other mere human beings. Remember the psalm-verse: 'The LORD is my light and my salvation: whom shall I fear? The LORD is the strength of my life; of whom shall I be afraid?'

Paul's fear and trembling were fear and trembling before God. They sprang from realization of the seriousness of his responsibility before God. To climb into this pulpit to declare God's holy Word – that is indeed something to move a wise man's heart to fear. Donald Cargill, the Covenanter, exclaimed from the foot of the gallows before his execution, 'Lord knows I go up this ladder with less fear and perturbation than ever I entered a pulpit to preach'. It would be a bad day for you, David, and a bad day for us too, if you were ever to feel quite at home in this pulpit and were able to stand here to preach without fear and trembling at the responsibility laid upon you. But I am very confident that you will never be among those preachers who know nothing of the fear and trembling to which Paul refers, because they have forgotten – or have never known – what it is they are meant to be doing.

III. In the third place, and lastly, let us look at verses 4 and 5. In verse 4 Paul continues: 'And my speech and my preaching were not in persuasive words of wisdom'. It was not that his speech had altogether lacked ordinary eloquence or that he had not tried to be as persuasive as he could without compromising his message. But he had not relied on cleverness of speech but on 'demonstration of the Spirit and of power'. Paul had known that, without the Holy Spirit's enabling him to speak God's Word truly and faithfully and without the Holy Spirit's enabling his hearers to hear aright and respond, all his speaking would have been in vain. But the Holy Spirit had indeed enabled him to speak and had indeed opened his hearers' hearts to the word spoken, creating in them true faith and a beginning of freedom to love God and neighbour. The 'demonstration of the Spirit and of power', of which Paul speaks, is, basically, the manifestation in human lives of the gift of the freedom to believe in Jesus Christ and so to be able to address the true God as 'Father' intelligently and sincerely, and to begin to think and act accordingly.

This verse calls you, David, to pray, 'Come, Holy Ghost', realizing that, without His work, your work will be in vain; to pray Him to sustain and increase your faith in Jesus Christ and so to grant you the freedom more and more to love God and your neighbour, so that in all you are and say and do there may be more and more clearly discernible, in spite of all your still remaining human weakness, the authenticity and integrity of a truly Christian human existence. And this verse calls you to pray Him to enable you so to study the Bible that you may hear what God wants to say to you and, through you, to us; and also to pray Him to enable those who listen to you to hear God's Word, to believe, and to receive the freedom and openness for God and fellow-man, which only God's Spirit can give. If you do so pray, your prayers will assuredly be answered, and, if these prayers are answered, your word and your preaching will indeed be 'in demonstration of the Spirit and of power'.

Verse 5 (the last verse of the text) indicates the purpose of what was described in verse 4. This was why Paul's speaking and preaching were not in persuasive words of human wisdom but in demonstration of the Spirit and of power, namely, in order that the Corinthian Christians' faith 'should not stand in the wisdom of men, but in the power of God'. It was in order that their faith might depend on nothing less than the almighty power of the eternal God.

Here then we see God's purpose and God's promise for this congregation here in Durham. What an amazing promise it is, a promise which should lift our spirits to new joy and hope and courage, the promise that we may be a congregation sustained in its life as a true, believing and witnessing Christian congregation by the almighty, saving power of God Himself! With such a promise, how can we not be of good courage?

In conclusion, let me try to draw together into two longish sentences the main things which this text has to say to David and to this congregation. It bids you, David, to concentrate your attention on Jesus Christ, never forgetting that He who is now the exalted Lord was once crucified for us sinners; to remember your own, and our, weakness and frailty; to recognize how serious a responsibility it is to have the duty of expounding God's holy Word and applying it to our lives; and to pray earnestly and without ceasing that the Holy Spirit may continue to dwell in you and to work in and through you God's good will. It bids us, the members and adherents of this congregation, to try to understand what our new minister is called by God to seek to do, and loyally and lovingly to try to help him to fulfil his calling faithfully; to remember that he, like every one of us, is beset with weakness; together with him to fix our attention steadily on Jesus Christ, crucified, raised, exalted, re-dedicating ourselves to His service, who is our only Saviour and Lord; and to pray – in joyful confidence that our prayers will be heard – that God may ever give us His Holy Spirit, so that our common life as a congregation and also our lives as individual Christian men and women may be lived in the power of God, to His glory and to the true good of all who dwell in this city and its neighbourhood and of all others with whom we have to do.

God bless you, David, and God bless this congregation! And may He bind you and us together in faithful love.

12

PREPARED FOR THE LORD[1]

> ... to make ready for the Lord a people prepared *for him.*
>
> (Luke 1.17.)

On this Third Sunday in Advent many Christians in many parts of the world will be reminded of the ministry of John the Baptist, the Forerunner, whose task it was to prepare the way for Jesus' own ministry, and of the continuing duty of the Church's ministers and teachers to try to help it both to be prepared to recognize and serve Christ as He comes now in the persons of His needy and afflicted brothers and sisters and also to be prepared for His glorious coming as our Final Judge. The words of our text are the last words of the message delivered before the birth of John to his father Zacharias. They foretell the nature of his work.

John's own ministry was a mixture of success and failure. Some of those, who flocked to hear him, later became followers of Jesus. These had indeed been made ready as a people prepared for the Lord. But many rejected both John and Jesus. John's message is summed up in Matthew 3.2 in the words, 'Repent ye; for the kingdom of heaven is at hand'. In that summary the latter part is logically prior. It is the news of the nearness of God's kingly intervention in mercy and salvation which is

[1] Sermon preached in Waddington Street United Reformed Church, Durham, on 16 December 1984.

the ground of the summons to repent. The kingdom of God is at hand: therefore repent! God was actually present for His people in the person of His Son, and was about to carry out His saving, healing, renewing work in Christ's earthly ministry, passion, resurrection and ascension. That was why John's call to repent was so urgent. The repentance to which he summoned his contemporaries included gladness at God's royal initiative, acknowledgement of, and sorrow for, sinfulness, a turning toward God in humble trust and acceptance of the assurance of His forgiveness, and readiness to let Him remake their lives in obedience to Him. It was by such repentance that those who heeded John's preaching were made ready for the Lord as a people prepared for Him.

And it is by repentance in response to God's grace in Jesus Christ, a repentance daily renewed, that we too have to be fashioned as a church into a people prepared for God, and – what, in particular, I want to dwell on this morning – fashioned as individual members into Christians who are prepared for the Lord, ready to be used by Him to His glory and the good of our neighbours. What does it mean for us to be 'prepared for him'?

I think I should be guilty of dereliction of duty, if I did not take this opportunity which has been given to me to try to bring this text right down to earth for us by attempting with God's help to see for myself, and to help you to see, something at least of what being prepared for God means for us concretely as Christians in Britain in Advent 1984 and in the weeks, months, years, immediately ahead of us.

Viscount Stockton spoke recently of his grief at the present deep and bitter divisions in our country. I think that all of us, if we love our country at all faithfully and if we are reasonably well informed and reflective, will understand and share Viscount Stockton's grief. The divisions are indeed cruelly deep and wide and bitter – such as no Christian could see without grief in any country of the world, least of all in the land where his home is and among the people who are his nearer neighbours.

What then does it mean for you and me, in this situation of anguish, to be prepared for God? prepared to be used by Him here and now for the good of our neighbours and prepared to render account to Him as our Judge, as we shall surely all of us have to do? There are a number of things which, in the light of Holy Scripture, must surely be said in reply to the question stated.

In the first place, if we have a real understanding of the grace of God in Jesus Christ, we cannot help being vividly conscious of our own sinfulness and so – at any rate, to some degree – purged of self-righteousness. And those who are even only just beginning to be freed from self-righteousness have a precious contribution to make to a country, which at the present time is being devastated by the arrogant, unquestioning self-righteousness of individuals and of groups. In a nation battered by the strident voices of those who foolishly declare that their opponents are alone to blame and pronounce their complacent condemnations of others as though they themselves were purer than the freshly fallen snow the Christian can at least bear witness to the truth that humanity is not made up of good and bad but only of sinners. You and I pray the words, 'If thou, Lord, shouldest mark iniquities, O Lord, who shall stand?' We can try to pray them with more and more understanding and sincerity, and to conform our thoughts and words and deeds more and more closely to our prayer. If we do, we shall hardly be impressed by the sight or sound of those who are continually challenging others to condemn this or that behaviour, but fail to ask themselves whether they are not in some measure responsible for what they so smugly condemn. Those who have studied the Sermon on the Mount will deplore all violence but will recognize that violence is committed in many different ways, all – and not only some – of which come under God's condemnation, and they will perceive the responsibility of those who wilfully provoke to violence. You and I will not forget our own deep involvement in the sickness of our society, which is the fertile soil in which violence and all manner of other foul things spring up and flourish and proliferate. We shall try then both to resist with all our might the temptation to self-righteousness on our own part and also, by words spoken or left unspoken, by deed and attitude, here and there, as we have opportunity, to do what we can to discourage self-righteousness in others.

In the second place, being aware that all are sinners, we shall be reluctant to witness the total victory of any individual or of any group. With total victory, or any thing approaching it at all nearly, only God can be trusted. We shall know, and, as we have opportunity, try to make others aware, that ruin and misery are certain to result, whenever fallible human beings forget that they are not God.

In the third place, since we know that all are sinners, we surely ought to be realistic enough to grasp the necessity of questioning critically what we hear and read and what we see on our television screens. We ought surely to reckon with the probability, indeed the certainty, that in a sinful society there will be many with a vested interest in misinformation. While we shall be profoundly grateful that there are a good many journalists in our country with a very high sense of responsibility for the truthfulness of what they publish, we shall also recognize that among those who have power over the means of mass-communication there are strong motives for misinformation at work, such as desire for party-political advantage, avarice, and greed for personal influence. And we shall be conscious of the wide variety of ways in which the public can be misinformed, ranging from the very crude to the very subtle and including direct falsehood, concealment, distortion, unfair selectivity in presenting facts, insinuation, to name but some. It is surely an important part of our preparedness for God that we should seek to assess as critically as possible all the information which comes to us. By so doing and by encouraging our neighbours to do likewise we shall be performing a valuable service to our country.

Fourthly, if we have a real understanding of the gospel, we shall know that, since Christ died for all and was raised up for all, and God loves and cares for all without exception, we must try with all our powers to respect the human worth and dignity of all, and to defend human worth and dignity where they are threatened or being trampled upon. And respect for the human dignity of the other man must surely include taking seriously his concerns and point of view and trying patiently to understand them. And, with regard to the dispute between the National Coal Board and the National Union of Mineworkers which has now gone on so long, respect for human dignity must surely incline us to give every support we can to those who are trying to get negotiations re-started and to make sure that, once re-started, they are pursued with patience and mutual respect, with readiness on both sides to engage in real conversation, and with steadfast determination not to break them off again till a negotiated and honourable settlement has been attained.

A fifth thing which should be said is that respect for the human dignity of all must include respect for the individual's conscience. Here a careful study of Romans 14.1–15.13 (the passage about the 'weak' and the 'strong') would help us; for, though the matters it refers to belong to a particular set of circumstances unfamiliar to us, it points very clearly and forcefully to the seriousness of causing an individual to act against his own conscience and so violate his own integrity as a person. If we understand this, it must surely be matter for deep concern and grief to us, both that any miner with a conscientious objection to the present strike should be compelled by intimidation or other pressure to participate in it, with consequent feelings of guilt, and also that any miner with a conscientious commitment to the strike should be forced, by the sufferings being endured by his loved ones as a result of the government's strategy against the miners, to go back to work, with consequent feelings of guilt for abandoning the course of action he judged to be right and for what must seem like a betrayal of his colleagues who are still holding out.

Sixthly, respect for the human dignity of all must surely mean for us resolving to bring what pressure we can to bear on our government to persuade it to give much higher priority to the fight against unemployment than it has so far done. Complacency in the face of the appalling waste of human lives, each one of them a once for all opportunity and only short, the waste of human strength and energy and skill and knowledge, all meant to be employed in the service of fellow-men, and the anguish of so many individuals and families in frustration and despair, is intolerable. The churches of this country are

179

right to challenge the government to face its responsibilities with regard to what is a still growing problem squarely and urgently and to afford some convincing evidence that it has some compassion.

Lastly, respect for the human worth and dignity of all must surely also mean for us opposing with steadfast determination those policies which are having the effect of making the gulf between the richest and the poorest in our country ever wider and wider. The world at the present time and the history of our own and other countries in the past afford only too much evidence of the miseries and disasters which result from the widening of the gap between rich and poor, and wise governments do what they can to narrow, not to widen, this chasm. And we, who are Christians who know that the God of the Bible has a special concern for the poorest and weakest and most vulnerable, must not fail to do all in our power to prevent the privileges of the rich and strong and secure in our land from being increased at their expense.

These are some of the things which being 'prepared for' the Lord must mean for us in our particular situation as Christians in a deeply divided country. May God grant that the Advent summons to repentance and readiness for Him may strike home to our hearts and to the hearts of many others in this land!